OVERCOMING
NEGATIVE
SELF-IMAGE

NEIL T. ANDERSON
DAVE PARK

Regal

From Gospel Light
Ventura, California, U.S.A.

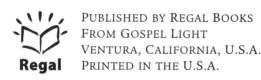

PUBLISHED BY REGAL BOOKS
FROM GOSPEL LIGHT
VENTURA, CALIFORNIA, U.S.A.
PRINTED IN THE U.S.A.

Regal Books is a ministry of Gospel Light, a Christian publisher dedicated to serving the local church. We believe God's vision for Gospel Light is to provide church leaders with biblical, user-friendly materials that will help them evangelize, disciple and minister to children, youth and families.

It is our prayer that this Regal book will help you discover biblical truth for your own life and help you meet the needs of others. May God richly bless you.

For a free catalog of resources from Regal Books/Gospel Light, please call your Christian supplier or contact us at 1-800-4-GOSPEL *or* www.regalbooks.com.

Cover and interior design by Robert Williams
Edited by Steven Lawson

Library of Congress Cataloging-in-Publication Data
Anderson, Neil T., 1942–
    Overcoming negative self-image / Neil T. Anderson and Dave Park.
        p. cm.
Includes bibliographical references.
    ISBN 0-8307-3253-5
    1. Self-esteem—Religious aspects—Christianity. I. Park, David,
1961– II. Title.
    BV4598.24.A53 2003
    248.4—dc21   2003004690

4   5   6   7   8   9   10   11   12   13   14   15   16   /   10   09   08   07   06

Rights for publishing this book in other languages are contracted by Gospel Light World-wide, the international nonprofit ministry of Gospel Light. Gospel Light Worldwide also provides publishing and technical assistance to international publishers dedicated to producing Sunday School and Vacation Bible School curricula and books in the languages of the world. For additional information, visit www.gospellightworldwide.org; write to Gospel Light Worldwide, P.O. Box 3875, Ventura, CA 93006; or send an e-mail to info@gospellightworldwide.org.

DEDICATION

Dan Roelofs knew who he was in Christ and modeled what it meant to be a child of God. I (Dave) first met Dan in Estes Park, Colorado, at a Student Venture conference at which he was speaking. It was obvious that Dan loved the Lord. Our conversation turned toward vision and fulfilling one's life dreams. I asked Dan, "What do you want to do with your life?" He paused for a moment and then said, "To be perfectly honest, I want to do what you and Neil do: tell people about Christ and help them find their identity and freedom *in Him.*" "Then why don't you do that?" I responded and offered Dan an internship with our ministry, which was still in its infancy. For the next two years, Dan traveled with us to our various conferences. His maturity and Christlikeness continued to grow as we shared two wonderful years together.

Fulfilling a promise to his wife, Tami, Dan took a youth pastor position and then felt called to plant a church. He and Tami had two wonderful boys and were very happy with the life God had given them. It even appeared that Dan had survived a bout with cancer. Then it returned. This time the melanoma traveled to his lymphatic system and then throughout his body. Dan had cancer on both of his lungs and on his liver. After conventional treatment had failed, the doctors told him to go home and straighten out his affairs.

Dan was secure enough in Christ to face death, but he humbly asked, "Lord, is it your will that I should die now?" In the face of a death sentence predicted by medical professionals, Dan had the peace to ask the Lord what His plans were. While battling cancer, Dan learned the meaning of surrender and deepened his understanding of his identity and position in Christ. Dan concluded, "This whole adventure isn't about getting rid of cancer; it is about knowing the Lord and doing His will." Through this incredible trial, Dan learned to live one day at a time to the glory and honor of God. This wonderful friend, pastor, husband and father is now seeing his Lord and Savior face-to-face.

Dan, we celebrate your life and sweet surrender to our Savior! Tami, we love you and suffer your loss with you.

"If you'll hold on to me for dear life," says God,

"I'll get you out of any trouble.

I'll give you the best of care

If you'll only get to know and trust me.

Call me and I'll answer, be at your side in bad times;

I'll rescue you, then throw you a party.

I'll give you a long life,

Give you a long drink of salvation!"

PSALM 91:14-16, *THE MESSAGE*

CONTENTS

ACKNOWLEDGMENTS

We want to thank you for trusting us enough to pick up this little book. We pray that the message will bless you and enrich your life in Christ. We want to thank our wonderful Lord and Savior for His love, mercy and grace, which is the transforming power in our lives. Without Him we would be nothing and have nothing to say. We also want to thank our wives, Joanne and Grace, for their patient support.

Finally, we want to thank the whole team at Regal Books: Bill Greig III, Kyle Duncan, Kim Bangs, Deena Davis, Nola Grunden, Steve Hahn, Elizabeth Wingate, Carole Maurer, Bayard Taylor, Rob Williams, KT Schuh and Steven Lawson. Working with you is like being part of a loving family. Thank you for making this book possible.

INTRODUCTION

Small books are fun to read! You do not feel as if you are making an overwhelming commitment. Finishing is a goal you can accomplish. However, writing a shorter manuscript instead of a longer one presents a different challenge. We want to explore the depths of who we are in Christ and how that solves our self-image problem—a topic that could fill volumes. Despite limited space, the message in this book nonetheless is indispensable for anyone who wants to live a liberated life in Christ.

Most people steer away from books that offer secrets for success or claim to be the key to solving all of their problems. We do, too. Such books usually fail to deliver on their promises. Why then is this book different? Knowing your identity and position in Christ is a fundamental gospel truth. Having "Christ in you, the hope of glory" (Col. 1:27) is germane to all that we are and do as Christians. We have helped hundreds of hurting people and have found one truth that they all fail to embrace: They have little or no understanding of who they are in Christ, nor do they comprehend what it means to be a child of God. This ignorance of spiritual truth results in negative or inflated beliefs about oneself and hampers one's walk with God.

Everybody has experienced the sting of rejection and worn labels that they cannot live up to or live with. Consequently, people do not inherently feel good about themselves. All counselors and pastors observe this type of negative self-image in the people with whom they work. The answer is not for people in this condition to pick themselves up by their own bootstraps and stroke their egos. That is a form of self-verification and it always falls short; but God has highly esteemed us, and therefore we can accept one another on the merits of Christ. Anyone can know who he or she is by the grace of God, which is realized through humility, not pride.

Our prayer is that the message of this little book will help you embrace the truth of what it means to be a child of God. We believe that our acceptance, security and significance can only be found in our eternal relationship with Him. Knowing who your heavenly Father is and who you are in relationship to Him is the basis for Christian living.

For the ease of reading, we will use the personal pronoun "I," without distinguishing between Neil Anderson and Dave Park. Names, titles and locations used in stories and testimonies are fictitious for the sake of anonymity, but the stories are true.

THE REJECTION
SYNDROME

*Try as we might by our appearance, performance or social status to
find self-verification for a sense of being somebody, we always come short of
satisfaction. Whatever pinnacle of self-identity we achieve soon crumbles under
the pressure of hostile rejection or criticism, introspection or guilt, fear or
anxiety. We cannot do anything to qualify for the by-product of being
loved unconditionally and voluntarily.*

MAURICE WAGNER

One day the DuPeire family received a phone call from their pastor.
He told them about a three-year-old boy who had been begging for
food at a local motel. Nobody was sure how long the child had
been left to fend for himself. The boy's mother, who had developed

cancer, had abandoned him, apparently thinking that little Matt would receive better care as a ward of the state.

The DuPeires adopted Matt as their own son. Living in his new home, he received the care and guidance that every child needs, yet feelings of abandonment haunted him for some time. Old programs ingrained in his mind from early childhood continued to gnaw away at his self-perception and shape his behavior. He ate every meal as though it might be his last. Sitting quietly at the dinner table was next to impossible. Matt would pile as much food on his plate as was humanly possible. He devoured every morsel that was placed before him.

Aware of Matt's behavior, his adoptive parents sought to correct his thinking. At the dinner table, they encouraged him to actually taste his food before he swallowed it, and later they showed him all the surplus food stored in the refrigerator and in the pantry. They thought that these acts would close the case of the child glutton, but they did not. A few days later Matt's adoptive mother entered his room and noticed a strange smell coming from his bed. At first she thought that one of the cats had an accident. Then she discovered a hidden tuna-fish sandwich under his pillow. Tuna was on the lunch menu three days earlier!

Matt's environment had completely changed, from insecurity to security, from rejection to acceptance, from abandonment to belonging. He was now a DuPeire. He had a new identity and a new family that promised to care for him, but the beliefs he held about himself and the world had not changed. It would take years to grow out of the old ways of thinking and acting.

Today Matt is a well-adjusted member of his adopted family. The transition he made from a dysfunctional family system to a healthier one is similar to the transition that every Christian makes at salvation. We have been transferred out of the kingdom of darkness to the kingdom of God's beloved Son (see

Col. 1:13). We have a new father and a new family, but our minds have already been programmed to live in the kingdom of darkness. To correct the negative images that we have of ourselves, we need to understand how we have learned to live in this fallen world.

THE KINGDOMS OF THIS WORLD

We were all born dead in our trespasses and sins (see Eph. 2:1). We had neither the presence of God in our lives nor the knowledge of His ways. Consequently, we all learned to live our lives independent of God. Like Matt, who as a child struggled to survive without parents, we learned to live without God. Our identity and perception of ourselves were programmed into our

> RENEWING OUR MINDS DOES NOT FULLY HAPPEN THE MOMENT WE RECEIVE CHRIST, AND IT CERTAINLY DOES NOT COME NATURALLY.

minds as we responded to the natural order of this fallen world. That is why Paul writes in Romans 12:2, "Do not conform any longer to the pattern of this world, but be transformed by the renewing of your mind" (*NIV*).

Renewing our minds does not fully happen the moment we receive Christ, and it certainly does not come naturally. There is no delete button that erases all the old tapes that have been recorded throughout our years of natural development. New believers and those who have failed to grow are like Matt was.

They tend to gravitate back to their old patterns of thinking and act accordingly.

The kingdoms of this world vary dramatically from one culture to another, as do the family systems within the cultures. Matt's previous family lived in the same community as his new family, but the culture was completely different. Culture and family systems are incredibly complex, and each has its own set of beliefs and values. Many sociologists and psychologists have devoted their professional lives to understanding these sociological systems. They attempt to explain why we do what we do as a result of the system in which we were raised. People, however, are not solely a product of their environment. Every one of us interprets the data and responds differently to the surroundings in which we were raised, because God gave each of us the capacity to think and make personal choices.

The kingdoms of this world are nothing like the kingdom of God. Living in this fallen world has many harsh realities such as poverty, disease and war. For the purpose of this chapter, let's consider rejection and the inevitable effect it will have on our self-perception and feelings. No matter how hard we try, we cannot avoid the rejection of others. Jesus lived a perfect life and the entire social and government establishment of that day rejected Him.

Several years ago, a 17-year-old girl drove a great distance to talk with me. I have never met a girl who had so much going for her. She was cover-girl pretty and immaculately dressed. She had completed 12 years of school in 11 years, graduating near the top of her class. As a talented musician, she had received a full-ride music scholarship to a Christian university. Her parents had given her a brand-new sports car for graduation. Few people have been endowed with so much.

After 30 minutes of conversation, it was easy to discern that her external presentation did not match the insecurities of her internal world. "Mary," I asked, "have you ever cried yourself to sleep at night because you felt inadequate and wished you were somebody else?"

Tears started to form in her eyes as she asked, "How did you know?"

I could ask almost anyone the same question at some time in his or her life and get the same response. The image we project to others often disguises how we really feel about ourselves. Most people cover up negative feelings about themselves in order to gain the acceptance of others. It is not always easy to live with someone who finds it difficult to live with himself or herself. So we wear a mask—even in church. Most people do not do it maliciously. We do it because we desire the acceptance and approval of others.

Many Christians are unaware that such negative self-perceptions are based on the values of this fallen world and that they reflect an inadequate understanding of the gospel. Genuinely speaking, appearance, performance and social status are the standards of this world. We use them to evaluate ourselves and to compare ourselves to one another.

In the kingdom of this world the natural man marginalizes unattractive, low-performance social misfits—there is no gushing nor offers of unconditional positive regard. Do attractive, smart and successful people experience the polar opposite? Obviously, some people lust over members of the opposite gender, such as supermodels and jocks, and members of the same gender become jealous. But how many years can you realistically stay attractive or strong? The huge fashion, fitness, health and beauty industries reveal that many believe their appearance is important to their sense of worth and enhances their prospects of being accepted. If that is not enough to prove our point, consider how many people in our current culture get Botox treatments to remove their wrinkles or cosmetic surgery to reshape their bodies.

When we focus on appearance, performance or social status, we fail to develop the lasting values of character that hold a relationship together. The result is a superficial life full of superficial relationships. External beauty cannot hide internal ugliness. Regardless of outer qualities and status, anything with a shallow base will eventually erode. Can you imagine the sting of rejection that must be felt when a woman discovers that a man "loved" only her body? Pity the man who is "loved" only for his money.

I am not suggesting that we should ignore our appearance, perform poorly or shun society. Rather, I am declaring that there are other standards by which we should ultimately evaluate ourselves—standards which are fair and available for all of God's children.

There is no such thing as unconditional love and acceptance in any human culture or family system. There is no way that we can live a perfect life and there is no way that we can please everyone. Consequently, the feelings of rejection are unavoidable. Generally speaking, we react to this fallen world by choosing one of three defensive postures (see figure 1).

THE TOP OF THE LADDER

Some people have an abundance of life endowments. A few who are born with very good genes or lots of money choose to use their assets to beat the system, and all too often their parents are the driving force behind their acts. The beat-the-system crowd recognizes the dog-eat-dog nature of our culture, and they do not want to be the ones that are eaten. So they do what they can to get to the top. They seek to establish names for themselves and take full advantage of their social status. They are going to gain their acceptance, security and significance via their own strength and resources.

Racism, sexism or any kind of elitism is perpetuated by people who want to maintain their favored status. They have exclusive

Figure 1

UNDERSTANDING REJECTION
Romans 15:7

**Think or feel
rejected and unloved**

↓

**Determine to please the significant other
and gain his or her approval**

↓

**More rejection comes resulting in
choosing one of three defense mechanisms**

↓   ↓   ↓

Beat the System*	Give In to the System*	Rebel Against the System*
↓	↓	↓
Accepts the system and competes and schemes to get ahead and become the significant other	Doesn't like the system and tries to cope and make do as a second-class citizen	Hates the system and fights social structures and often behaves or dresses in objectionable ways
↓	↓	↓
Results in superficial relationships as performance and appearance diminish with age	Seeks an identity and sense of belonging but poor self-image affects the ability to relate and compete	Results in more rejection and causes others to defend the system they reject
↓	↓	↓
Inability to express feelings, emotional insulation, perfectionism, worries, insecurity	Feelings of worthlessness, inferiority, subjectivity, introspection, self-condemnation	Undisciplined, irresponsible, self-hating, bitter
↓	↓	↓
Has little need for God and struggles with lordship	Needs God or something but struggles with trust	Sees God as a tyrant and rebels against Him

*Note: The family system is the most significant in early development, followed by school and society in general.

clubs and form social communities that only welcome the privileged and the best. The tragedy and utter selfishness of those who climb to the top at the expense of others was revealed to the world when Enron collapsed. Enron's executives were living the high life, and every new employee wanted to be just like them. They saw the yachts and expensive homes, but what they did not see was the emotional insulation and perfectionism that was driving them. Pride comes before a fall, but in this case, the fall affected thousands of investors who lost their retirement and financial security. In the end, the world's system cannot deliver.

There are many ways in which people try to beat the system. They will attempt to leverage their exceptional appearance, talents, intellect or athleticism. Consider the tragic life of Lyle Alzado. He was one of the fiercest competitors who ever played the game of football. As a defensive end, he personified the Raiders's mystique. With his incredible strength and speed, Alzado was like a heat-seeking missile. He locked on to whoever had the pigskin and usually left the poor fellow drilled into the ground. Twice he made the Pro-Bowl team.

In college Lyle was not sure he could make it to the NFL, since he only weighed 195 pounds. That is not enough weight to be a defensive lineman in the National Football League. So Lyle decided to take steroids, and he became a monstrous 300-pound defensive machine. His decision to take steroids brought him the success and fame he desired, but only for a short time. The steroids probably caused the brain cancer that ended his life. Lyle Alzado died at 43 years of age. His life was literally cut in half.[1]

THE SEDUCTIVENESS OF THE SYSTEM

Most people will never be a part of the jet set, be a corporate executive, win a beauty pageant, play professional sports or achieve something considered significant by the world's standards—and we know it. We tend to buy into the negative side of the worldly success formula where appearance, performance and status equal acceptance, security and significance. We cannot compete with those who are more talented or gifted, so we give in to the system. I asked a high school student, "Suppose there's a boy on your campus who has a frail body and matted hair. He stumbles when he walks and stutters when he talks. He could use some help with personal grooming, and he struggles to make average grades. Does he have any hope for acceptance, security and significance?" He thought for a moment, and answered, "Probably not." The world's system of measurement can be quite hostile, even in the best of countries.

> ## IF FOUR PEOPLE AFFIRMED YOU AND ONE CRITICIZED YOU, WHICH ARE YOU INCLINED TO BELIEVE?

Studies have revealed that in American homes an average child receives ten negative or nonaffirming statements for every positive or affirming statement. In school, where teachers are taught to know better, an average student receives seven negative or nonaffirming statements for every positive or affirming statement. A study wanted to find what it would take to erase the effect of one negative statement, and it found out that it took at least four affirming statements on average. If four people affirmed you and one criticized you, which are you inclined to believe or at least think the most about? No wonder most people struggle with a poor identity and a negative sense of worth.

Several years ago when I was a pastor, I put the words "inadequacy," "inferiority," "insecurity," "guilt," "worry" and "doubt" on a card. When people sought counseling, I pulled out the card and asked if they could identify with any of those words. Forty-nine Christians said all six and one mentioned only four. Something is radically wrong. These people were beaten down by the system, and they seemed to be ignorant of their spiritual heritage in Christ. Many struggled with the idea of God, believing that their poor state in life was His fault.

THE REBELLION OF PEOPLE

I was right across the street from Columbine High School when Dylan Klebold and Eric Harris took the lives of a teacher and several classmates. They were part of the school's trench-coat mafia, exemplifying rebellion against the system. They underscored their defiance by dressing and behaving in objectionable ways. Their actions suggested that they did not want or need anyone's love, but in actuality they did—as we all do. This kind of disenfranchised segment of society has been growing since the 1960s. Those who sought to beat the system were their nemesis. Bullied and badgered, they finally snapped, as have several others on high school campuses around the nation. The system is sick. Everybody loses in the end. No wonder John wrote:

> Do not love the world [system], nor the things in the world. If anyone loves the world, the love of the Father is not in him. For all that is in the world, the lust of the flesh and the lust of the eyes and the boastful pride of life, is not from the Father, but is from the world (1 John 2:15-16).

THE EXAMPLE OF SOLOMON

If anyone had a chance to beat the system, it was King Solomon. He was the king of Israel when the nation was at its greatest prominence. He occupied the highest of human positions. He had power, wealth and any woman that he pleased. If a meaningful life is the result of appearance, performance and status, Solomon would have experienced it, but he did not.

Something was missing from Solomon's life. Therefore, he sought to find purpose and meaning in life without God. God had said to Solomon, "I have given you a wise and discerning heart, so that there has been no one like you before you, nor shall one like you arise after you" (1 Kings 3:12). What did Solomon conclude? "Meaningless! Meaningless! Utterly meaningless! . . . Everything is meaningless!" (Eccles. 1:2, *NIV*).

No human being will ever be afforded the same opportunity that Solomon had for self-verification. The proud have not learned from his experience. They agree with the poet, "I am the master of my fate, the captain of my soul."[2] Oh, no, we are not! God never designed the soul to function as master. We either serve God or mammon. Often when we serve the latter, we are deceived into thinking we are serving ourselves. Millions of people try to climb the ladder of success, only to discover when they get to the top that their ladder is leaning against the wrong wall!

THE OVERCOMERS OF THIS WORLD

Moving the ladder over to the right wall often requires some dramatic intervention. Dave Dravecky was a pitcher for the San Francisco Giants. He was a wealthy star performer with rugged good looks. From the world's perspective, he had it all. At the peak of his career, Dave was diagnosed with cancer in his pitching arm.

He underwent surgery to have the cancer removed. The doctors were sure that he would never play the game of baseball again, but they underestimated his drive to achieve. He not only returned to the game, but he also won the first game he pitched after rehabilitation.

The very next game, however, he broke his arm. This time the doctors could not save it. Dave had to have his arm and shoulder amputated. How important was Dave Dravecky's pitching arm to him? He writes:

> My arm was to me what hands are to a concert pianist, what legs are to a ballerina, what feet are to a marathon runner. It is what the people cheer me for, what they paid their hard-earned money to see. It is what made me valuable, what gave me worth, at least in the eyes of the world. Then suddenly my arm was gone.[3]

Was Dave Dravecky's life over because he lost his arm? Was he no longer able to achieve any sense of worth? Was this man, who was a somebody in the world of sports, now a nobody? Dave had been a pitcher, but suddenly he was not. Dave Dravecky pitched, but that is not who he is or was. Dave is a child of God, and as with most of us, it took something dramatic for this truth to settle fully in his conscious self. He has accomplished more for the cause of Christ with one arm than he ever did with two. He realized that who he is goes far beyond his ability to throw a baseball. He continues:

> When I came home from the hospital, I realized that all my son, Jonathan, wanted to do was wrestle with me and play football on the lawn. All my daughter, Tiffany, wanted was to hug me, and all Jan, my wife, wanted was to have her husband back. They didn't care whether

I had an arm or not. . . . It was enough that I was alive and that I was home.[4]

Dave Dravecky did not beat the world's system. Actually, it beat him, but he overcame it by finding the unconditional love and acceptance of God.

Joni Eareckson Tada had all the appearance, performance and status needed to compete in this world when she dove into shallow water and broke her neck. She could have been somebody in the world system, but she became somebody far greater in Christ, and from her wheelchair, she has touched the lives of millions all over the world. Moses was no good for God in the pharaoh's court, but he was good after he lost all of his earthly advantages. Chuck Colson was no good for God in the United States White House, but he was in prison.

THE INVASION OF THE CHURCH

After I explained the rejection syndrome—succumbing to the world's standards in order to be accepted—to a Sunday School class of adults, a man asked, "Which one of those defenses is right?" I hope his poor wife survived the embarrassment. To some extent, the world's system has invaded every church, and many Christians are not sure what their identity is and fail to achieve a legitimate sense of worth. Some Christians even question whether they should have any sense of worth. They falsely believe that being nothing and doing nothing are signs of true humility, because being someone and doing something would draw attention to themselves. Such shame-based thinking is not consistent with the grace of God. Jesus did not die for nothing, and bearing fruit is the means by which our heavenly Father is glorified (see John 15:8). David Meyers wrote:

To sense divine grace . . . is to be liberated from both self-protective pride and self-condemnation. To feel profoundly affirmed, just as I am, lessens my need to define my self-worth in terms of achievements, prestige, or material and physical well-being. It is rather like insecure Pinocchio saying to his master, Geppetto, "Papa, I am not sure who I am. But if I'm all right with you, then I guess I'm all right with me."[5]

GOING DEEPER

1. What old programs (feelings of rejection) are ingrained in your mind? How do they affect your self-image today?
2. Have you ever tried to compete with the world's system? How? What was the result?
3. What are the elements of self-verification that you or your family have used to establish your identity and sense of worth?
4. If you need to move your ladder to a different wall, how are you going to do this?

CHAPTER 2

THE ORIGINAL DESIGN

The deepest questions we ever ask are directly related to our hearts' greatest needs and the answers life gives us shape our image of ourselves, of life, and of God. Who am I? The romance whispers we are someone special, that our heart is good because it is made from someone good; the arrows tell us we are a dime a dozen, worthless, even dark and twisted, dirty.

BRENT CURTIS AND JOHN ELDREDGE, *THE SACRED ROMANCE: DRAWING CLOSER TO THE HEART OF GOD*

Years ago a pastor asked if I would counsel his daughter. Nancy was not going to make it through her senior year of high school unless something changed. Everyone was impressed with her beauty and talent. Through most of her teenage years she received lots of affirmation for her looks and her ability to sing. Still she struggled with a negative self-image.

Understandably, Nancy had focused on her appearance and performance—these are what people complimented most. However, such compliments and the drive to maintain what is being praised (in this case, looks and musical ability) snag people in a seductive trap. Many adults have thus been ensnared, so we can hardly expect a child like Nancy to be mature enough to handle the applause and adulation of others.

I asked Nancy who she would be if she were in an automobile accident, damaged her vocal cords and scarred her face. "I wouldn't be anybody," she replied. With that I started to help her build a biblical foundation of who she was in Christ, and God orchestrated an unusual set of events. She had to stay home one weekend and fulfill some family responsibilities, which really upset her. I do not know to this day how I found out about it, but that Friday night she totally abdicated her responsibility and got drunk.

The next week I asked her about her weekend. "Everything went fine," she said.

"Friday night was fine?" I asked.

She said it was. I paused, and then I looked her right in the eye and said, "Nancy, I just want you to know that I wouldn't do anything to spy on you or pry into your private life; but I happen to know that Friday night didn't go well. What I want you to know is that it doesn't make any difference how I perceive you. You are a child of God, and I love you and accept you just as you are."

She did not just cry; she bawled for 15 minutes.

When she finally regained her composure, I asked, "What were you thinking during that time?"

"I just hate myself," she said.

That was her turning point. Eighteen years of performance-based living started to crumble under the unconditional love of God.

Figure 2

ORIGINAL CREATION
Genesis 1—2

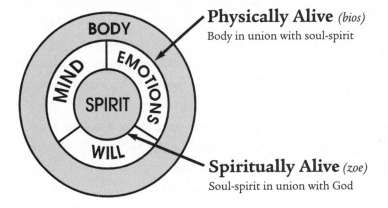

Physically Alive *(bios)*
Body in union with soul-spirit

Spiritually Alive *(zoe)*
Soul-spirit in union with God

1. Significance—Man had a divine purpose (Gen. 1:28).
2. Safety and security—All of man's needs were provided for (Gen. 1:29).
3. Belonging—Man had a sense of belonging (Gen. 2:18).

bios = The soul is in union with the body.
zoe = The soul is in union with God.

A negative self-image is inevitable when the self is the creator of it. We have another image, one that we were created in. If we are going to build a true image of ourselves—one that is lasting, fair and available for all—we need to start with what it means to be created in the image of God. Genesis 1:26 and 2:7 read:

Then God said, "Let Us make man in Our image, according to Our likeness." Then the LORD God formed man of dust from the ground, and breathed into his nostrils the breath of life; and man became a living being.

This combination of clay and divine breath constituted the first person created in God's image. Figure 2 graphically shows the component parts that made up Adam's basic nature. God is a Spirit and we are created in His image, but Adam had a physical body as well as a soul and spirit. Some theologians understand the soul and the spirit to be essentially the same, while others understand the human soul to be different from the human spirit. For the sake of our discussion, we will explain our basic nature as being comprised of an inner person and an outer person. We will refer to ourselves as having a material self and an immaterial self. The soul or soul-spirit is what sets humanity apart from the animal kingdom, which operates out of instinct. Because we are created in the image of God, we can think, feel and choose.

Having a material self, we can relate to the world around us through the five senses: taste, touch, smell, hearing and sight. When God breathed the breath of life into Adam's nostrils, Adam became physically *and* spiritually alive.

PHYSICAL LIFE

To be physically alive means the soul or soul-spirit is in union with our own body. To die physically means that we separate from our own mortal body. In the Bible, to die means "to be separate from,"[1] and to be alive means "to be in union with."[2] Paul wrote that to be absent from the body is to be present with the Lord (see 2 Cor. 5:8).

Obviously, our core identity encompasses more than our physical body, because our body will be left behind when we physically die and we (the inner person who is the essential "I") will be present with the Lord. Therefore, to build a concept of self around only our physical appearance and traits is woefully inadequate. However, our immaterial self needs our material self to function in this physical world.

For example, your physical brain is like the hardware of a computer system and your immaterial mind is like the software.

The hardware cannot perform any meaningful function without software, and the software needs the hardware in order to fulfill its purpose. The brain can only function according to how it has been programmed. We can do little to change the physical nature of our brains, and this is why the major emphasis of Scripture is

> IN ORDER TO RESTORE
> A DAMAGED SELF-IMAGE,
> WE HAVE TO BE TRANSFORMED
> BY THE RENEWING OF
> OUR MINDS.

on the software. In order to restore a damaged self-image, we have to be transformed by the renewing of our minds, which is part of our immaterial self. Our hope cannot lie in the eternal preservation of our physical bodies, because they are in a state of decay. Paul wrote, "Therefore we do not lose heart, but though our outer man is decaying, yet our inner man is being renewed day by day" (2 Cor. 4:16).

I was listening to a man who owns and operates a workout gym. He is a physically impressive person with well-developed muscles. He remarked, "I hope I don't get a new body when I go to heaven, because I've worked so hard to form this one!" The good news is that we do get a new body when we die. His comment revealed that his identity and self-concept were wrapped up in his physical appearance, and he was doing everything he could to stop the decaying process. Think of the millions of people who undergo plastic surgery or take some other drastic measures to prolong the inevitable.

It is appointed for men to die once and after this comes judgment (Heb. 9:27).

SPIRITUAL LIFE

Adam was also created to be spiritually alive. To be spiritually alive means that our soul or soul-spirit is in union with God. Had Adam and Eve never sinned, they could have lived forever, both physically and spiritually. "The LORD God commanded the man, saying, 'From any tree of the garden you may eat freely; but from the tree of the knowledge of good and evil you shall not eat, for in the day that you eat from it you shall surely die'" (Gen. 2:16-17). They did eat from the forbidden tree, and they did die. Initially they did not die physically, but they did die spiritually. Their souls were no longer in union with God. Physical death would be a consequence as well, but for Adam it did not come for more than 900 years.

Adam's sin affected every one of His descendants. Paul wrote, "Through one man sin entered into the world, and death through sin, and so death spread to all men, because all sinned" (Rom. 5:12). We were all born into this world physically alive, but spiritually dead (see Eph. 2:1). Although we retain some aspects of the original design, the image of God has been shattered; and there is humanly no way that we can recapture it or correct it. Without the Spirit of God within us, we are incomplete and empty. John Eldredge, in his book *The Journey of Desire*, states this emptiness and lack of connection with our creator:

Something awful has happened; something terrible. Something worse, even, than the fall of man. For in that greatest of all tragedies, we merely lost paradise—and with it, everything that made life worth living. What happened since is unthinkable: we've gotten used to it. *We're broken in to the idea that this* is just the way things are. The people who walk in great darkness have adjusted their eyes.[3]

The good news is we have been made alive together with Christ. This is the gospel, but many people have been so deeply affected by the Fall and the resultant world system that they continue to live as they always have. They have grown accustomed to the darkness and find it difficult to believe that they are indeed accepted by their creator.

God is in the process of reestablishing a fallen humanity and repairing our damaged self-image. He wants to restore in us what He originally created in Adam and meet our deepest needs, which are the "being" needs, beginning with spiritual life. Jesus said, "I came that they might have life" (John 10:10). This spiritual life defines our identity. "But as many as received Him, to them He gave the right to become children of God" (John 1:12). To understand what else God is trying to restore, consider what Adam and Eve had before the Fall.

SIGNIFICANCE

In the original creation, Adam and his descendants were given a divine purpose for being here.

> Then God said, "Let Us make man in Our image, according to Our likeness; and let them rule over the fish of the sea and over the birds of the sky and over the cattle and over all the earth, and over every creeping thing that creeps on the earth." And God created man in His own image, in the image of God He created him; male and female He created them (Gen. 1:26-27).

Adam did not have to search for significance because he was significant. Significance was not a need; it was an attribute of creation. There was no emptiness in his heart, and he did not hunger and thirst after righteousness, because he was without sin and consciously in the presence of God. Adam did not know what it was like to feel insignificant.

Satan wanted dominion over this world, but God gave that responsibility to Adam and his descendants. At that time, Satan was not the god of this world. To become so, he had to orchestrate the downfall of Adam and Eve. Having succeeded in doing so, he became the rebel holder of authority. Jesus referred to Satan as the ruler of this world. To overcome the effects of the Fall, Jesus would have to destroy the works of Satan—this is another reason why our heavenly Father sent Jesus (see 1 John 3:8).

SAFETY AND SECURITY

Adam and Eve were also safe and secure. Genesis 1:29 records:

> Then God said, "Behold, I have given you every plant yielding seed that is on the surface of all the earth, and every tree which has fruit yielding seed; it shall be food for you; and to every beast of the earth and to every bird of the sky and to every thing that moves on the earth which has life, I have given every green plant for food."

They could eat of the tree of life and live forever. They were safe and secure in the presence of God.

Since the tragic events of September 11, 2001, many Americans are experiencing a greater sense of insecurity. The United States president proposed and Congress has created a Department of Homeland Security to deal with the threat of terrorism and help people with their insecurities. The effort is commendable, but it will not be enough. We cannot humanly control the movements of everybody and seal every border.

> They have healed the brokenness of My people superficially, saying, "Peace, peace," but there is no peace (Jer. 6:14).

There will be no *external* peace in this fallen world until the Lord comes back, because we have no ability or right to control all the inhabitants. The peace we have in Christ refers to an *internal* order, not the external order of this world. Jesus said, "Peace

> ## THE PEACE WE HAVE IN CHRIST REFERS TO AN *INTERNAL* ORDER, NOT THE EXTERNAL ORDER OF THIS WORLD.

I leave with you; My peace I give to you; not as the world gives, do I give to you. Let not your heart be troubled, nor let it be fearful" (John 14:27).

SENSE OF BELONGING

Adam also had a sense of belonging in the Garden of Eden. He was God's special creation, and He enjoyed an intimate relationship with Him; but there was more. "The LORD God said, 'It is not good for the man to be alone; I will make him a helper suitable for him'" (Gen. 2:18). Adam and Eve had a sense of belonging not only with God but also with each other. They were naked and unashamed.

They had nothing to hide. Their bodies had no dirty parts. They could have an intimate sexual relationship with each other in the presence of God. Sex was God's idea for procreation as well as pleasure. They were to be fruitful and multiply, and fill the earth with godly descendants who would rule over His creation.

Most Christians do not feel like Adam and Eve felt before the Fall. Many put on a good face, but they come to church with a tarnished image. Many wear a mask hoping others will not sense what is going on inside.

Suppose I had the opportunity to get to know you—I mean really know you—intimately. If I did, would I like you? I think I would, but not because of any great virtue of my own. The God who lives within me motivates me to reach out to the hurting, neglected and lost souls with His love and compassion. I have seen feelings of abandonment and rejection disappear when confronted by the unconditional love and acceptance of our heavenly Father. Josh McDowell writes, "If ever you put a price tag on yourself, it would have to read 'Jesus.' His death on the cross was payment for our sins. You are 'worth Jesus' to God because that's what he paid for you."[4]

In his book *Shaking the Foundations*, Paul Tillich adds:

You are accepted. You are accepted, accepted by that which is greater than you. . . . Do not try to do anything now; perhaps later you will do much. Do not seek for anything, do not perform anything now; do not intend anything. Simply accept the fact that you are accepted. If that happens we experience grace.[5]

GOING DEEPER

1. What was God's divine purpose for Adam and his descendants?
2. How does your physical life differ from your spiritual life?
3. What does it mean to have a sense of significance?
4. What does it mean to have a sense of belonging?

SHATTERED IMAGE

Our hearts are restless until they find rest in Thee.

SAINT AUGUSTINE

In the late nineteenth century, a circuit preacher was making his rounds from one settlement to another on the western frontier of America when he came upon a young Greek immigrant orphan who had been abandoned by a raiding party. The preacher had no choice but to take the boy along. Peter turned out to be an incorrigible kid, and it became obvious that the preacher could not do his work and provide for him.

The preacher heard about a Christian family named Smith that had recently settled near one of his routes. He asked them if they would prayerfully assume responsibility for the boy, and they agreed. The Smith family had a son named Sammy who was about Peter's age, and they became the best of friends, even though Peter continued to be difficult.

They warned the boys not to go near the swamp because everyone believed it was contaminated. Peter would not listen. One day he managed to work his way through the barbed wire fence and go swimming. He must have scratched himself on the rusty fence, because he became infected and fell deathly ill. He was quarantined, lest others would catch what he had.

Peter's life hung in the balance, and Sammy could only watch and pray as he peered through an open door. Then one afternoon, Mr. and Mrs. Smith had to make a trip to town to get some supplies. They warned Sammy not to go near Peter, but when they came home, they found the two boys fast asleep in each others arms. Nobody understands the providence of God, but in this case, Peter got well and Sammy got sick. In fact, Sammy died.

The circuit preacher had all but forgotten about Peter when several years later he was making his rounds near the Smith home. Recalling the incident, he decided to make a visit to see what happened to the little orphaned Greek boy. As he approached the farm, he recognized Mr. Smith, but he did not recognize the young man by his side. "By the way, whatever happened to that incorrigible kid I dropped off a few years back?" he asked.

Mr. Smith reached up and put his arms around the shoulders of the young man and said, "I want you to meet Peter Smith. We adopted him."

According to another Peter—the apostle—the same act of grace has happened to every believer:

But you are a chosen race, a royal priesthood, a holy nation, a people for *God's* own possession, that you may

proclaim the excellencies of Him who has called you out
of darkness into His marvelous light; for you once were
not a people, but now you are *the people of god*; you had
not received mercy, but now *you have received mercy* (1 Pet.
2:9-10, emphasis added).

What did Peter Smith think about himself after being abandoned on the western frontier? I suspect it was not much different from what Adam and Eve felt about themselves after the Fall.
The idyllic setting in the garden was shattered and so was their
self-image. The effects of the Fall were dramatic, immediate and
far-reaching, infecting every subsequent member of the human
race, as pictured in figure 3.

Figure 3

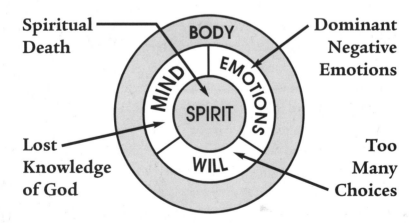

EFFECTS OF THE FALL
Genesis 3:8—4:9

Spiritual Death

Dominant Negative Emotions

Lost Knowledge of God

Too Many Choices

BODY · EMOTIONS · SPIRIT · WILL · MIND

SPIRITUAL DEATH

The most immediate consequence for Adam and Eve was spiritual death. Their union and intimacy with God was severed and they were separated from Him. They were expelled from the Garden of Eden, and a cherubim with a flaming sword was stationed at the entrance "to guard the way to the tree of life" (Gen. 3:24). Some people believe the angel was preserving a way back to God as His plan of redemption unfolded.

Adam's sin resulted in spiritual death for all his descendants, because all have sinned (see Rom. 5:12; 1 Cor. 15:21-22). According to the French mathematician and philosopher Blaise Pascal, "there is a God-shaped vacuum in the heart of every man, which cannot be filled by any created thing, but only by God the Creator, made known through Jesus Christ."[1] The point is we are incomplete without Christ. God never created Adam and his descendants to live independent of Him.

Apart from Christ we are like a new automobile coming off the production line in Detroit. Suppose a factory representative were to fly in from Australia an Aborigine who had never seen modern civilization and ask him to determine the purpose of the car. It might be the most beautiful thing he had ever seen. He would certainly conclude that it was an object of beauty, perhaps a piece of art. But that is not the purpose of the automobile. Then he might sit in the driver's seat and conclude that it was made for comfort. Never before had he sat in something so cushy. But that is not the purpose of the automobile.

If a representative were to turn the key in the ignition just enough to turn on the quadraphonic sound, he would know: this car was a theater of sound. It was made for entertainment. If the representative were to turn on the lights, it would become a source of light! If he, excited now, were to accidentally honk the horn, it would become a noise-making device. The man might be enamored by this remarkable machine, but he would never discover its purpose, which was transportation, because it was out of gas.

So are we without Christ. There is no way we can determine who we are or fulfill our calling without Christ. The natural person is like a lightbulb without electricity.

MENTAL IMPAIRMENT

As a result of the Fall, there were immediate noticeable changes in Adam. The first was the effect spiritual death had upon his mind. He lost a true perception of reality and the idea of knowing was no longer relational. This became evident when he tried to hide from an omnipresent God.

It reminds me of the time when my two girls were about three and five years old. They loved to play Hide-and-Seek. I would stay upstairs and bury my face in a pillow and start counting. As soon

> ADAM AND EVE HAD A DISTORTED CONCEPT OF GOD AND THEMSELVES, AND SO DO WE.

as I said, "Ready or not, here I come," they proceeded to laugh and giggle uncontrollably. I never had any problem finding them. They did not seem to realize that their laughter revealed their hiding place.

Adam and Eve had a distorted concept of God and themselves, and so do we. Paul explains why: "They are darkened in their understanding and separated from the life of God because of the ignorance that is in them due to the hardening of their hearts" (Eph. 4:18, *NIV*). They were darkened in their understanding because they were separated from the life of God.

It takes some spiritual insight to understand that the idea of knowing is relational and knowing the truth is tied into our relationship with God. In Genesis 4:1, "Adam knew Eve his wife, and she conceived" (*KJV*). Today we do not use the word "know" that way. To the natural person, knowledge is a collection of data disconnected from the source of knowledge. The natural person can know something *about* God, but not know Him personally. God is the ultimate reality and there is no knowledge apart from Him. Wisdom is seeing life from God's perspective, but the natural person can only see life from his or her perspective.

A natural man does not accept the things of the Spirit of God, for they are foolishness to him; and he cannot understand them, because they are spiritually appraised (1 Cor. 2:14).

Anyone who could understand the Greek language and culture must have been astonished when John wrote, "The Word [*logos* in Greek] became flesh" (John 1:14). To the Greek philosopher, logos represented the highest form of philosophical knowledge. To say that the Word became flesh meant that knowledge or wisdom was incarnated; i.e., it took on a human form. Jesus is the Word. He is the truth. We cannot separate the truth from His personhood. Having a true knowledge of God, which was lost in the Fall, is now possible again through a personal relationship with Jesus Christ. We can know Him and who we are alive in Christ, because every born-again believer has the mind of Christ within them (see 1 Cor. 2:16).

Knowledge apart from God makes people arrogant, but love builds us up (see 1 Cor. 8:1). Making knowledge an end unto itself is the primary problem with Western education. Such an emphasis distorts the actual purpose for which knowledge was intended. Paul writes, "The goal of our instruction is love from a pure heart and a good conscience and a sincere faith" (1 Tim. 1:5). The truth (Christ and His Word) was intended to set us free and set us on the path of conforming to the image of God. Jesus said, "By this all men will know that you are my disciples, if you have love for one another" (John 13:35).

I read somewhere that people referred to handicapped children as "children of God" during the Dark Ages. I used to think that was a nice euphemism, but there may have been another reason:

> Nine runners took off in the 100-yard dash. The leader in the race fell while he was running and skinned his knee. Then an amazing sight took place. All the other kids ran past the young man who had been out in front, but when they heard him crying they all stopped and went back to comfort him. One of the little girls kissed his knee to make it feel better. After they helped him up they all linked arms. The children finished the race with arms linked together. The crowd gave them a standing ovation, cheering and crying for those incredible giving kids.[2]

DAMAGED EMOTIONS

Adam and Eve's understanding was darkened and they became fearful and anxious. The first emotion expressed by fallen humanity was fear (see Gen. 3:10). Fear of anything other than God is mutually exclusive to faith in God. Why is the fear of God the beginning of wisdom? How does the fear of God expel all other fears?

As I was writing the book *Freedom From Fear*[3] with my colleague Rich Miller, I became aware that we are living in an age of anxiety. People all over the world are paralyzed by fear of anything and everything but God. Anxiety disorders are the number one mental health problem of the world. Chuck Colson said, "For the church in the West to come alive, it needs to resolve its identity crisis, to stand on truth, to renew its vision . . . and more than anything else, it needs to recover the fear of the Lord."[4]

Adam and Eve felt guilty and tried to hide from God. Plagued by a sense of shame, they tried to cover up. When dominated by guilt and shame, self-disclosure is not likely to happen.

After the Fall, Adam and his descendants also felt depressed and angry. Cain brought his offering to God, and God was displeased with it.

> So Cain was very angry, and his face was downcast. Then the Lord said to Cain, "Why are you angry? Why is your face downcast? If you do what is right, will you not be accepted? But if you do not do what is right, sin is crouching at your door; it desires to have you, but you must master it" (Gen. 4:5-7, *NIV*).

Cain was angry and depressed, because he did not do what was right. This illustrates a biblical principle: *You do not feel your way into good behavior; you behave your way into good feelings.* Jesus said, "If you know these things, you are blessed if you do them" (John 13:17). The world is experiencing a blues epidemic in this age of anxiety. Depression is called the common cold of mental illness. Depression has doubled from 1985 to 1995 in America, and there was a tenfold increase in the last century.[5]

CHOICES TO MAKE

Adam and Eve's sin affected their will to choose. In the Garden of Eden they could only make one wrong choice. Everything they wanted to do was okay, except eat from the tree of the knowledge of good and evil (see Gen. 2:16-17).

> APART FROM THE HOLY SPIRIT IN OUR LIVES, THE GREATEST POWER WE POSSESS IS THE POWER TO CHOOSE.

Because of the Fall, we are confronted every day with myriad good *and* bad choices. Apart from the Holy Spirit in our lives, the greatest power we possess is the power to choose. We can decide to pray or not pray, read the Bible or not read the Bible, go to church or not go to church. We can opt to walk according to the flesh or according to the Spirit. The fact that nobody can make all of the right choices reveals the power of the law, which actually stimulates us to do what it was intended to prohibit.

> For while we were in the flesh, the sinful passions, which were aroused by the law, were at work in the members of our body to bear fruit for death (Rom. 7:5).

If you tell a child he can go here but not there, where does he want to go? There! The fruit appears to be more desirable when it is forbidden.

- The law is not contrary to the promises of God, but it cannot give life (see Gal. 3:21).
- Telling people that what they are doing is wrong does not give them the power to stop doing it.

We are "servants of a new covenant, not of the letter [of the law], but of the Spirit; for the letter kills, but the Spirit gives life" (2 Cor. 3:6).

GLARING NEEDS

1. The sense of unconditional love and acceptance has been replaced by feelings of rejection; therefore, we have a need to belong.
Ever since Adam and Eve's sin alienated them from God and introduced strife into human relationships, we have experienced a deep need to belong. This basic need is the driving force behind peer pressure. We can lead people to Christ, but if our churches cannot provide them with friendships, we will lose them. One study reported that it takes an average of seven social connections within six months to keep a visitor coming back to church. The spiritual union of Christian fellowship (*koinonia* in Greek) meets a critical need and is essential for our growth.

2. Innocence was replaced by guilt and shame; therefore, we all have a need for a legitimate sense of worth.
Having an identity crisis and struggling with a negative self-image have plagued humanity in every generation and in every culture. Trying to reestablish our lost identity and shattered sense of worth is not clearly understood by people in many of our churches.

We tend to identify ourselves by what we do. Some people have suggested that men get their identity from their work, because God said to Adam, "By the sweat of your face you shall eat bread" (Gen. 3:19). By the same reasoning, women should get their identity from bearing and raising children, because God said, "In pain you shall bring forth children" (Gen. 3:16). Those verses are part of the curse. What would happen if the man were to lose his job or could not work anymore? What would happen if a woman were to never marry or could not have children?

How can we have or how can we acquire a legitimate sense of worth, one not based on the curse? By exercising spiritual gifts? I do not think so, because God has not gifted everyone in the same way. God equalized that by "giving more abundant honor to that member which lacked" (1 Cor. 12:24). Do our talents give us a greater sense of worth? It would be very unfair for some if that were true, because God has given some one talent, others two and some five (see Matt. 25:14-30). We might be tempted to conclude that only the five-talented Christian can have any sense of worth. But that simply is not true. In fact, the supergifted and supertalented face the risk of focusing too much on their abilities and not enough on their growth in character.

Do we have a greater sense of worth if we are very intelligent? Here is what the Bible answers: "Has not God made foolish the wisdom of the world?" (1 Cor. 1:20). Highly intelligent people are more easily tempted to lean on their own understanding. Gifts, talents and intelligence are God-given capacities that can be used to build up the Church, but they are not the basis for our identity and sense of worth.

3. Dominion was replaced by weakness and helplessness; therefore, we have a need for strength and self-control.
Without God, we attempt to meet this need by our own strength and resources. Power is what we want, so we try to get it by leveraging our assets. Some people attempt to reach a dominating position through physical strength, while others use their intellect, money or sex. For some people, having personal power is not enough; they desire to manipulate others. There is nobody more insecure than a controller, because the object of his or her faith is self. He or she likes to play God.

The fruit of the Spirit is not spouse control, staff control or environmental control; it is self-control (see Gal. 5:23). The Christian finds his or her strength in God. As the apostle Paul did, we also need to discover that "power is perfected in weakness" (2 Cor. 12:9).

> # THE FRUIT OF THE SPIRIT IS NOT SPOUSE CONTROL, STAFF CONTROL OR ENVIRONMENTAL CONTROL; IT IS SELF-CONTROL.

Satan tempts us to live our lives independent of God, and he tries to take advantage of our basic and legitimate needs. The question is, Are these needs going to be met by the world, the flesh and the devil, or are they going to be met by God, who promises to meet all our needs "according to His riches in glory in Christ Jesus" (Phil. 4:19)?

The needs most wonderfully met in Christ are the following being needs:

IN CHRIST

I Am Accepted

John 1:12	I am God's child.
John 15:15	I am Jesus' chosen friend.
Rom. 5:1	I have been holy and accepted by God (justified).
1 Cor. 6:17	I am united with the Lord and one with Him in spirit.

1 Cor. 6:20	I have been bought with a price—I belong to God.
1 Cor. 12:27	I am a member of Christ's body, part of His family.
Eph. 1:1	I am a saint, a holy one.
Eph. 1:5	I have been adopted as God's child.
Eph. 2:18	I have direct access to God through the Holy Spirit.
Col. 1:14	I have been bought back (redeemed) and forgiven of all my sins.
Col. 2:10	I am complete in Christ.

I Am Secure

Rom. 8:1-2	I am free from punishment (condemnation).
Rom. 8:28	I am assured that all things work together for good.
Rom. 8:31	I am free from any condemning charges against me.
Rom. 8:35	I cannot be separated from the love of God.
2 Cor. 1:21	I have been established, anointed and sealed by God.
Col. 3:3	I am hidden with Christ in God.
Phil. 1:6	I am sure that the good work that God has started in me will be finished.
Phil. 3:20	I am a citizen of heaven.
2 Tim. 1:7	I have not been given a spirit of fear but of power, love and a sound mind.
Heb. 4:16	I can find grace and mercy in time of need.
1 John 5:18	I am born of God and the evil one cannot touch me.

I Am Significant

| Matt. 5:13 | I am the salt and light for everyone around me. |
| John 15:1,5 | I am a part of the true vine, joined to Christ and able to produce much fruit. |

John 15:16	I have been handpicked by Jesus to bear fruit.
Acts 1:8	I am a personal witness of Christ.
1 Cor. 3:16	I am God's temple where the Holy Spirit lives.
2 Cor. 5:17	I am at peace with God, and He has given me the work of making peace between Himself and other people. I am a minister of reconciliation.
2 Cor. 6:1	I am God's coworker.
Eph. 2:6	I am seated with Christ in the heavenlies.
Eph. 2:10	I am God's workmanship.
Eph. 3:12	I may approach God with freedom and confidence.
Phil. 4:13	I can do all things through Christ who strengthens me.[6]

GOING DEEPER

1. Has the idyllic setting of your "garden" ever been shattered?
2. What do you fear?
3. How are the attributes of unconditional love, innocence and dominion, which were evident in creation, related to you?
4. How can you find acceptance, security and significance in Christ?

THE WHOLE GOSPEL

You're done with that old life. It's like a filthy set of ill-fitting clothes you've
stripped off and put in the fire. Now you're dressed in a new wardrobe.
Every item of your new way of life is custom-made by the Creator, with his
label on it. All the old fashions are now obsolete. Words like Jewish and
non-Jewish, religious and irreligious, insider and outsider, uncivilized and
uncouth, slave and free, mean nothing. From now on everyone is
defined by Christ, everyone is included in Christ.

COLOSSIANS 3:9-11, *THE MESSAGE*

A newly adopted child found himself in a big mansion. His new
father whispered in his ear, "This is yours, and you have a right
to be here. I have made you a joint heir with my only-begotten

son. He paid the price that set you free from your old taskmaster, who was cruel and condemning. I purchased it for you because I love you."

The young boy could not help but question this incredible gift. *This seems too good to be true. What did I do to deserve this?* He wondered. *I have been a slave to other people's expectations all my life, and I have never measured up. What have I done to earn such a privilege?*

The boy was deeply grateful, however, and began to explore all the rooms in the mansion. He tried out some of the tools and appliances. Many other adopted children lived in the mansion as well, and the boy began to form relationships with his new brothers and sisters.

He especially enjoyed the buffet from which they freely ate. Then it happened! While turning away from the buffet table, he knocked over a stack of glasses and a valuable pitcher crashed to the floor and broke. Suddenly he began to think, *You clumsy, stupid kid! You will never get away with this. What right do you have to be here anyway? You better hide before someone finds out, because they will surely throw you out!*

At first, he was caught up with the wonder of living in the mansion with a whole new family and a loving father, but now he was confused. Old tapes laid down in early childhood began to play again in his mind. He was filled with guilt and shame. The self-condemning thoughts continued: *Who do you think you are: some kind of privileged character? You do not belong here anymore; you belong in the basement! My old taskmaster was right about me— I don't belong here, because I have done nothing to earn it and now I have failed again.* With his mind filled with such thoughts, the boy descended into the basement.

The cellar was dreary, dark and despairing. The only light came from the open door at the top of the long stairs from which he came. He heard his father calling for him, but he was too ashamed to answer.

The boy was surprised to find others in the basement, too. Upstairs people talked with each other and joined in to carry out daily projects that were fun and meaningful. In the basement, however, nobody talked. They were too ashamed. Although no one liked it there, most felt that the basement was where he or she really belonged. Each one did not see how he or she could ever walk in the light again. If he or she did, others would see the imperfections.

Occasionally one of the new brothers or sisters who remained upstairs would come to the door and encourage those in the basement to come back up—that brother or sister would even announce that a place was prepared for everyone who would return. Some brothers and sisters were not very helpful. They would scold everyone in the basement, which only worsened the situation.

Not everyone had the same reason for staying in the basement. Some, like the boy, thought that they deserved to be there— that they had been given a chance, but did not measure up to the expectations of their new father. Others did not think they could climb the stairs. The task seemed impossible. Even if they mustered up the strength to try, the staircase of expectation only grew longer and steeper. They could not reach the top by their own strength and resources, and they were too proud to ask for help.

Some of the basement dwellers would muster the courage to go upstairs for a short time, but they never stayed long enough to resolve their conflicts and learn the truth that would enable them to remain. So they returned to the basement.

Others stopped trying, because they feared the possibility of being rejected. They would think, *If they only knew the real me, they would surely throw me out. I can't be a hypocrite and pretend any more. I am not worthy of their love.*

When the newly adopted child first arrived in the basement, he groped around in the darkness, trying to find a way to survive.

The longer he stayed, the more the memory of what it was like to live upstairs faded and the hope of ever returning diminished. Those old tapes from early childhood caused him to question the love of this new father, and he began to wonder whether he was ever actually adopted.

The noise of people having fun upstairs irritated him. He remembered the light upstairs being warm and inviting, but now, whenever the basement door opened, the light seemed penetrating and revealing. He recalled hearing his adopted father say that most people loved the darkness rather than the light, for their deeds were evil.

The boy made a few halfhearted attempts to return to the light, but eventually he found a dark corner to lie in. To survive, he ate grubs and moss off the damp walls.

Then one day a shaft of light penetrated his mind, and reason returned. He began to think, *Why not throw myself on the mercy of this person who calls himself my father? What do I have to lose? Even if he makes me eat the crumbs that fall from the table, it would be better than this.* So, risking the possibility of rejection, he climbed the stairs and faced his father with the truth of what he had done.

"Father," he said, "I knocked over some glasses and broke a pitcher." Without saying a word, his father took him by the hand and led him into the dining room. To the boy's utter amazement, his father had prepared a banquet for him!

"Welcome home, son," his father said. "There is no condemnation for those who are in Christ Jesus!"

Oh, the deep, deep love of Jesus and the matchless grace of God! "In love He predestined us to adoption as sons through Jesus Christ to Himself, according to the kind intention of His will, to the praise of the glory of His grace, which he freely bestowed on us in the Beloved" (Eph. 1:4-6).

If people fully understood our heavenly Father's unconditional love and acceptance, they would never find themselves in the basement of rejection and self-condemnation. In order to comprehend our place in the family of God, we have to understand the whole gospel and what Jesus came to do for us.

His Steps

Mary was pregnant before she was married. She could have been stoned to death under Jewish law and probably would have if an angel had not intervened. Jesus was born of very humble means and grew up in the home of a carpenter who was not wealthy.

Jesus was not from the tribe of Levi, so the priesthood was not a possibility. He had no social standing that would give Him any advantage with Rome's leaders or in the Jewish community. He did not seem to have any material possessions. Isaiah prophesied, "He has no stately form or majesty that we should look upon Him" (53:2). Jesus had no special physical appearance or social status, and His performance brought nothing but rejection from the establishment. How could He have any sense of worth? Certainly the constant abuse and rejection He received should have shattered it. All He could claim was that He and His heavenly Father were one—of course, that is all He needed. That claim by Jesus is all we need as well.

Jesus gave us an example that we should follow in His steps (see John 13:15). He showed us how, with a spiritual life, a person can live in this fallen world. What He modeled was a life totally dependent upon His Father. The first Adam—mentioned in Genesis—failed to do this. Eve was deceived and believed a lie. The first Adam willfully chose to act independent of God. Jesus—the last Adam—said, "I can do nothing on My own initiative. I live because of the Father. I proceeded forth and have come from God, for I have not even come on My own initiative, but He sent Me. The words that I say to you I do not speak on My own, but the Father abiding in Me does His work" (John 5:30; 6:57; 8:42; 14:10).

The ultimate test came after a 40-day fast. Jesus, led by the Holy Spirit, went into the wilderness, where Satan tempted Him. The serpent said, "If you are the Son of God, command that these stones become bread" (Matt. 4:3). Satan wanted Jesus to use His divine attributes independent of the Father to save Himself. Jesus replied, "Man shall not live on bread alone, but on every word that proceeds out of the mouth of God" (Matt. 4:4). Near the end of His earthly ministry, Jesus prayed, "Now they know that everything you have given me comes from you" (John 17:7, *NIV*).

HIS PURPOSE

As was the first Adam, Jesus was born both physically and spiritually alive. By this we mean that both Adam and Jesus came into being by the Spirit of God—Adam being created of dust and Jesus being born of a virgin. As was Adam, Jesus was tempted in every way; but unlike the first Adam, He never sinned. He never

> IN THE FALL, ADAM AND
> EVE LOST THEIR SPIRITUAL
> LIFE—JESUS CAME TO GIVE
> BACK THAT LIFE.

lost His spiritual life because of any act He committed. He kept His spiritual life pure all the way to the cross. There He bled and died, taking the sins of the world upon Himself. He committed His spirit into the Father's hands as His physical life ended (see

Luke 23:46). In the Fall, Adam and Eve lost their spiritual life—Jesus came to give back that life. Jesus said, "I came that they might have life, and might have it abundantly" (John 10:10).

John declared, "In Him was life; and the life was the light of men" (John 1:4). Notice that light does not produce life. Life produces light. Jesus said, "I am the bread of life" (John 6:48), and "I am the resurrection and the life; he who believes in Me will live even if he dies" (John 11:25). In other words, those who believe in Jesus will continue to live spiritually even when they die physically. Jesus said, "I am the way, and the truth, and the life" (John 14:6). The ultimate value is not in our physical life that is temporal, but it is in our spiritual life that is eternal.

The Whole Gospel

Jesus is the Messiah who came to die for our sins, and if we pray to receive Him, our sins will be forgiven and we will go to heaven when we die. Presenting the gospel that way can result in two discrepancies in our understanding.

First, many people would understand only half of the benefits of the gospel. Let's look at this a bit closer. If you want to save dead people and you have the power to do so, what would you do? Give them life? However, if that is all you do, they will only die again. To save dead people (and we were all born dead in our trespasses and sins), you would have to do two things. First, you would have to cure the disease that caused them to die. The Bible declares, "The wages of sin is death" (Rom. 6:23). So Jesus went to the cross and died for our sins. Is that the whole gospel? No! Finish the verse, "But the free gift of God is eternal life." Thank God for Good Friday, but what Christians celebrate every spring on Easter Sunday is the Resurrection. When we leave the Resurrection out of the gospel presentation, people understand themselves to be nothing more than forgiven sinners instead of the redeemed saints who they truly are "in Christ." In their self-perception, they are the same person; except now they are forgiven. That is not true. In Christ, we are new creations (see 2 Cor. 5:17).

There is a second problem with the above gospel presentation. It gives people the impression that eternal life is something they get when they die, and that is a misrepresentation. Read 1 John 5:11-12: "And the testimony is this, that God has given us eternal life, and this life is in His Son. He who has the Son of God has the life; he who does not have the Son of God does not have the life." If we do not have spiritual (eternal) life before we die physically, we can only look forward to hell.

THE DIFFERENCE MAKER

The difference between the first and last Adam is the difference between life and death. Paul wrote in 1 Corinthians 15:22, "As in Adam all die, so also in Christ all shall be made alive." Being spiritually alive is most often portrayed in the New Testament with the prepositional phrases "in Christ," "in Him" or "in the Beloved." These are some of the most repeated prepositional phrases in the New Testament, occurring nearly 40 times in the book of Ephesians alone. Being "in Christ" means that our souls are in union with God. Every believer can say with Paul, "I have been crucified with Christ; and it is no longer I who live, but Christ lives in me; and the life which I now live in the flesh I live by faith in the Son of God, who loved me, and delivered Himself up for me" (Gal. 2:20).

For every biblical passage that teaches "Christ in you," there are ten passages that teach that you are "in Christ." It is also the primary basis for Paul's theology:

For this reason I have sent to you Timothy, who is my beloved and faithful child in the Lord, and he will remind you of my ways which are *in Christ*, just as I teach everywhere in every church (1 Cor. 4:17, emphasis added).

As you therefore have received Christ Jesus the Lord, so walk *in Him*, having been firmly rooted and now being built up *in Him* (Col. 2:6-7, emphasis added).

Let's look at the first five verses of Ephesians:

Paul, an apostle of Christ Jesus by the will of God, to the saints who are at Ephesus, and who are faithful in Christ Jesus: Grace to you and peace from God our Father and the Lord Jesus Christ. Blessed be the God and Father of our Lord Jesus Christ, who has blessed us with every spiritual blessing in the heavenly places in Christ, just as He chose us in Him before the foundation of the world, that we should be holy and blameless before Him. In love He predestined us to be adopted as sons through Jesus Christ to Himself, according to the kind intention of His will.

Now consider how these verses relate to who we truly are in Christ:

1. You are called a saint (v. 1).
2. You are called faithful (v. 1).
3. You have grace from God the Father and from Jesus Christ (v. 2).
4. You have peace from God the Father and from Jesus Christ (v. 2).
5. You have already received every spiritual blessing (in Him) in heavenly places (v. 3).
6. You were chosen by God to be (in Him) before He made the world (v. 4).

7. You have been made holy (in Him) (v. 4).

8. You have been made blameless (in Him) (v. 4).

9. You are loved by God (v. 4).

10. You have been adopted into His family, because He chose to do it (v. 5).

We encourage you to read the rest of Ephesians to see the blessings of being alive in Christ. The problem is, as human beings, we do not see it. Therefore, Paul prays, "I pray that the eyes of your heart may be enlightened, so that you will know what is the hope of His calling, what are the riches of the glory of His inheritance in the saints" (Eph. 1:18).

NEW BIRTH

Our natural heritage offers no guarantee of a future spiritual heritage. John wrote, "Yet to all who receive him, to those who believed in his name, he gave the right to become children of God—children born not of natural descent, nor of human decision or a husband's will, but born of God" (1:12-13, *NIV*). The passage is true even if you are the child of a famous evangelist.

When the name Billy Graham became nationally known, so many tourists showed up each day at the Graham home just outside of Asheville, North Carolina, that eventually the family purchased several acres of mountain land and built a log house where they could have some privacy. Since Dr. Graham was away preaching most of the time, his wife, Ruth, oversaw the construction, taking along the couple's oldest child, Franklin, who was intrigued by the workers, their tools and especially their cigarettes.

"I caught on that if I ran quick enough when they pitched a cigarette," Franklin later recounted, "the butt would still be lit. I would grab one and puff away, thinking no one would notice."[1]

Ruth Graham would often notice, grab the cigarette out of his mouth and lecture him on the evils of smoking. The workmen seemed to enjoy the sideshows, so they kept pitching half-smoked cigarettes in Franklin's direction. A bad habit began early.

In an effort to break Franklin of smoking, Ruth borrowed a pack of cigarettes, pulled one out and handed it to Franklin. "Now light it and smoke it," she snapped, "and be sure to inhale." She wanted Franklin to get sick, hoping he would lose his desire to smoke. After the second cigarette, his face turned green, and he ran to the bathroom and threw up. But he stubbornly came back for more, and by the end of the night he had finished all 20.

After many rebellious years passed, Franklin, by then a young man, yielded his life to Jesus Christ. He was surprised to discover that his taste for cigarettes was as strong as ever. He genuinely wanted to quit smoking, but he could not seem to kick the habit. He later explained that he would wake up at night with "an absolutely overwhelming—almost terrifying—desire for a cigarette. I wanted to smoke so bad that I couldn't think of anything else. It intensified with each passing minute. Throughout the day, the yearning for a cigarette grabbed me like the jaws of a junkyard dog."[2]

He finally shared his struggle with his friend Roy Gustafson. "Roy, I quit smoking, but I don't think I can hold out. I just don't think I have the power to say no any longer," Franklin said.

"Oh, you don't, huh?" replied Roy, looking up from a hamburger. "Why don't you just get down on your knees and tell God He's a liar."

"What? I can't do that!"

Roy quoted 1 Corinthians 10:13: "No temptation has overtaken you except such as is common to man; but God is faithful, who will not allow you to be tempted beyond what you are able, but with the temptation will provide the way of escape, that you may be able to endure it."

Then looking at Franklin, he said bluntly, "You need to tell God He's a liar. You claimed that verse and it didn't work."

"I'm not going to call God a liar," said Franklin, alarmed. "Besides, I haven't claimed that verse yet!"

"You haven't?" said Roy, sounding shocked. "Why don't you then?"[3]

Franklin did claim that verse. And it did work.

How can the son of the world's most famous evangelist have spiritual problems? Simple! He was born dead in his trespasses and sins (as we all are), and he learned (as we all have) to live his life independent of God. Consequently, we have all adopted the standards of this world. Salvation transfers us out of the kingdom of darkness and into the kingdom of God's beloved Son (see Col. 1:13). We are no longer in Adam; we are in Christ, but we have

> THERE IS NO SUCH THING AS INSTANT MATURITY. IT WILL TAKE TIME TO CONFORM TO THE IMAGE OF GOD.

retained many of the old ways of thinking about ourselves. There is no such thing as instant maturity. It will take time to conform to the image of God. Our tattered self-image is being renewed as we are being transformed by the renewing of our minds.

Success comes in *cans* and failure in *cannots*. Believing you can takes no more effort than believing you cannot. So why not believe that you *can* walk by faith in the power of the Holy Spirit; that you *can* resist the temptations of the world, the flesh and the devil; and that you *can* grow as a Christian. It is your choice. The following 20 Cans of Success, gleaned from God's Word, will expand your knowledge of God. Building your faith by internalizing the truth of God's word will lift you from the miry clay of the *cannots* to the *cans* of righteous living.

TWENTY CANS OF SUCCESS

1. Why should I say I cannot when the Bible says I can do all things through Christ, who gives me strength (see Phil. 4:13)?

2. Why should I worry about my needs when I know that God will take care of all my needs according to His riches in glory in Christ Jesus (see Phil. 4:19)?

3. Why should I fear when the Bible says God has not given me a spirit of fear but of power, love and a sound mind (see 2 Tim. 1:7)?

4. Why should I lack faith to live for Christ when God has given me a measure of faith (see Rom. 12:3)?

5. Why should I be weak when the Bible says that the Lord is the strength of my life and that I will display strength and take action because I know God (see Ps. 27:1; Dan. 11:32)?

6. Why should I allow Satan control over my life when He that is in me is greater than he that is in the world (see 1 John 4:4)?

7. Why should I accept defeat when the Bible says that God always leads me in victory (see 2 Cor. 2:14)?

8. Why should I lack wisdom when I know that Christ became wisdom to me from God and God gives wisdom to me generously when I ask Him for it (see 1 Cor. 1:30; James 1:5)?

9. Why should I be depressed when I have hope and can recall to mind God's loving-kindness, compassion and faithfulness (see Lam. 3:21-23)?

10. Why should I worry and be upset when I can cast all my anxieties on Christ, who cares for me (see 1 Pet. 5:7)?

11. Why should I ever be in bondage, knowing that there is freedom where the Spirit of the Lord is (see 2 Cor. 3:17)?

12. Why should I feel condemned when the Bible says there is no condemnation for those who are in Christ Jesus (see Rom. 8:1)?

13. Why should I feel alone when Jesus said He is with me always and He will never leave me or forsake me (see Matt. 28:20; Heb. 13:5)?

14. Why should I feel as if I'm cursed or have bad luck when the Bible says that Christ rescued me from the curse of the law that I might receive His Spirit by faith (see Gal. 3:13-14)?

15. Why should I be unhappy when I, like Paul, can learn to be content, whatever the circumstances (see Phil. 4:11)?

16. Why should I feel worthless when Christ became sin for me so that I might become the righteousness of God (see 2 Cor. 5:21)?

17. Why should I feel helpless in the presence of others when I know that if God is for me, who can be against me (see Rom. 8:31)?

18. Why should I be confused when God is the author of peace and He gives me knowledge through His Spirit who lives in me (see 1 Cor. 2:12; 14:33)?

19. Why should I feel like a failure when I am more than a conqueror through Christ, who loved me (see Rom. 8:37)?

20. Why should I let the pressures of life bother me when I can take courage knowing that Jesus has overcome the world and its problems (see John 16:33).

GOING DEEPER

1. Have you ever felt as if you were living in the basement while other believers were enjoying the fellowship of God and others? When did this happen and why?

2. What is the difference between the first Adam and the last Adam?

3. How do the verses that show who you truly are in Christ impact you?

4. Which of the 20 Cans of Success are evident in your life, and which ones do you need to start believing in order to live a full productive life?

CHAPTER 5

A NEW IDENTITY

A saint is never consciously a saint; a saint is consciously dependent on God.

OSWALD CHAMBERS

God creates out of nothing. Wonderful, you say. Yes, to be sure, but He does what is still more wonderful: He makes saints out of sinners.

SØREN KIERKEGAARD

Slavery in the United States was abolished by the Thirteenth Amendment on December 18, 1865. How many slaves were there December 19? In reality, none; but many still lived like slaves, because they never learned the truth. Others heard the good news, but continued living as they had always been taught and thus maintained their negative self-image.

The plantation owners were devastated by this proclamation of emancipation. We're ruined! Slavery has been abolished. We've lost the battle to keep our slaves. But their chief spokesman slyly responded, Not necessarily. As long as these people think they're still slaves, the proclamation of emancipation will have no practical effect. We don't have any legal right over them anymore, but many don't know it. Keep your slaves from learning the truth, and your control over them will not even be challenged.

But what if the news spreads?

Don't panic. We have another barrel on our gun. We may not be able to keep them from hearing the news, but we still have the potential to deceive the whole world. They don't call me the father of lies for nothing. Just tell them that they misunderstood the Thirteenth Amendment. Tell them that they are going to be free, not that they are free already. The truth they heard is just positional truth, not actual truth. Someday they may receive the benefits, but not now.

But they'll expect us to say that. They won't believe us.

Then pick out a few persuasive ones of their own who are convinced that they're still slaves and let them do the talking for you. Remember, most of these newly freed people were born slaves and have lived like slaves all their lives. All we have to do is to deceive them so that they still think like slaves. As long as they continue doing what slaves do, it will not be hard to convince them that they must still be slaves. They will maintain their slave identity because of the things they do. The moment they try to confess that they are no longer slaves, just whisper in their ears, "How can you even think you are no longer a slave when you are doing things that slaves do?" After all, we also have the capacity to accuse the brethren day and night.

Years later, many slaves have still not heard the wonderful news that they have been freed, so naturally they continue to live the way they have always lived. Some slaves have heard the good news, but they evaluate it by what they are presently doing and feeling. They reason, I'm still living in bondage, doing the same things I have always done. My experience tells me that I must not be free. I'm feeling the same way I was before the proclamation, so it must not be true. After all, your feelings always tell the truth. So they continue to live according to how they feel, not wanting to be hypocrites.

One former slave hears the good news, and receives it with great joy. He checks out the validity of the proclamation, and finds out that the highest of all authorities originated the decree. Not only that, but it personally cost that authority a tremendous price, which he willingly paid so that the slaves could be free. As a result, the slave's life is transformed. He correctly reasons that it would be hypocritical to believe his feelings and not the truth. Determined to live by what he knows to be true, his experience begins to change rather dramatically. He realizes that his old master has no authority over him and does not need to be obeyed. He gladly serves the one who set him free.[1]

A TRUE PROCLAMATION OF EMANCIPATION

The gospel is our proclamation of emancipation. We were all slaves to sin, and "it was for freedom that Christ set us free" (Gal. 5:1). Every born-again child of God is alive and free in Christ, but how many are living free and productive lives? How many really understand what it means to be a child of God? The world system has conditioned us to believe that we are what we do. So we

> # EVERY BORN-AGAIN CHILD OF GOD IS ALIVE AND FREE IN CHRIST, BUT HOW MANY ARE LIVING FREE AND PRODUCTIVE LIVES?

are plumbers, carpenters or homemakers. Some distinguish themselves according to race, religion, culture or social standing. The kingdom of God has no such distinctions and a different means by which we should identify ourselves. The apostle Paul explains:

> Do not lie to one another, since you laid aside the old self with its evil practices, and have put on the new self who is being renewed to a true knowledge according to the image of the One who created him—a renewal in which there is no distinction between Greek and Jew, circumcised and uncircumcised, barbarian, Scythian, slave and freeman, but Christ is all, and in all (Col. 3:9-11).

Also, there is no sexism in the kingdom of God. In Galatians 3:28, Paul leaves no doubt: "There is neither male nor female." That does not abolish sexual identity in the physical realm; rather, it means that every born-again believer is a child of God regardless of sex. The point: What we do, where we live or what social class we represent does not determine who we are. Who we are determines what we do, and that is why the Holy Spirit bears witness with our spirit that we are children of God.

It is also false reasoning to ask, "What experience must I have in order for this to be true?" The only experience needed occurred more than 2,000 years ago, and the only way we can enter into it is by faith. We do not make anything true by our experience or by our belief. What God says is true whether we believe it or not. Truth is not conditioned by our belief, but we— as human beings—are. We choose to believe what God says is true and then walk accordingly by faith and works. Trying to make our faith true by our experience will lead to endless searching and fruitless efforts.

We do not labor in the vineyard with the hope that God may some day love us. God loves us and that is why we labor in the vineyard. We do not do what we do with the hope that God may some day accept us. God accepts us and that is why we do what we do. Knowing that we are new creations in Christ frees us up to be and do all that God has called us to be and do. We cannot consistently behave in a way that is inconsistent with what we believe about ourselves. So who are we? According to 1 John 3:1-3, we are children of God and believing this truth leads to our purification:

> See how great a love the Father has bestowed on us, that we would be called children of God; and such we are. For this reason the world does not know us, because it did not know Him. Beloved, now we are children of God, and it has not appeared as yet what we shall be. We know that when He appears, we shall be like Him, because we shall see Him just as He is. And everyone who has this hope fixed on Him purifies himself, just as He is pure.

SINNER OR SAINT?

With worldly thinking, we conclude that believers are all sinners, because we all sin. Since we all write, are we all *writers*? The Bible does not identify believers as sinners, it identifies believers as saints who sin. A saint is literally a holy person, but the designation does not describe our growth in character. It defines our position in Christ. For example, Paul's salutation in 1 Corinthians 1:2 reads:

> To the church of God which is at Corinth, to those who have been sanctified in Christ Jesus, saints by calling, with all who in every place call upon the name of our Lord Jesus Christ, their Lord and ours.

Paul does not say that we are saints by hard work. He clearly declares that we are saints by calling. Because of the unholy conduct of many believers, the word "saint" has often been reserved for those who exhibit superior character and behavior. The Bible, on the other hand, identifies all believers as saints (see Rom. 1:7; 2 Cor. 1:1; Phil. 1:1). In the *King James Version*, believers are called saints, holy ones or righteous ones more than 200 times. In contrast, unbelievers are called sinners more than 300 times. Clearly the term "saint" is used in Scripture to refer to the believer and the term "sinner" is used in reference to the unbeliever.

Although the New Testament gives us plenty of evidence that the believer sins, it never clearly identifies the believer as a sinner. What about Paul's reference to himself as foremost of sinners (see 1 Tim. 1:15)? Despite the use of the present tense by the apostle, several arguments make it clear that his self-description is a reference to his preconversion opposition to the gospel. He indeed *was* the chief of all sinners, because nobody opposed the plan of God with more zeal than he did. There are several reasons why this passage is looking back at what Paul was before he came to Christ.

First, the reference to himself as a sinner is in support of the first half of the verse, "Christ Jesus came into the world to save sinners" (1 Tim. 1:15). The reference to "the ungodly and sinners" a few verses earlier (v. 9), along with other New Testament uses of the term "sinners," shows that the sinners whom Christ came to save were outside of salvation rather than believers who can still choose to sin.

Second, Paul's reference to himself as a sinner is immediately followed by the statement "And yet . . . I found [past tense] mercy" (v. 16), which clearly points to the past occasion of his conversion. Paul continued to be amazed by the mercy of God toward himself, who had been the worst sinner.

A similar present self-evaluation based upon the past is seen when the apostle says, "I am [present] the least of the apostles, who am not fit to be called an apostle, because I persecuted the church of God" (1 Cor. 15:9). Because of his past action, Paul considered himself unworthy of what by God's grace and mercy he presently was: an apostle who was in no respect "inferior to the most eminent apostles" (2 Cor. 12:11).

Third, although declaring that he is the worst sinner, the apostle at the same time declares that Christ had strengthened him for the ministry having considered him "faithful" or trustworthy for the ministry to which he was called (v. 12). The term "sinner," therefore, does not describe him as a believer; rather, it is used in remembrance of what he was before Christ took hold of him.

The only other places in Scripture that could be referring to Christians as sinners are in James. The first—"Cleanse your hands, you sinners" (4:8)—is one of ten verbal commands urging anyone who reads this general epistle to make a decisive break with the old life. This is best understood as calling the reader to repentance and therefore salvation. The second use of "sinner" is in James 5:19-20 and appears to have a similar reference to unbelievers. The sinner is to be turned from the error of his ways and thus be saved from death. Since this most likely means spiritual death, it suggests that the person is not a believer. In both places, James uses the term "sinner" as it was particularly used by Jews to refer to anyone who disregarded the law of God and flouted standards of morality.

The fact that these sinners are among the people addressed by James does not necessarily mean they are believers. Scripture teaches that unbelievers can be among the saints (see 1 John 2:19), as there surely are today in our churches. Referring to them as sinners fits the description of those who have not come to repentance nor accepted faith in God, since the rest of Scripture clearly identifies believers as saints who still have the capacity to sin.[2]

> AS BELIEVERS, WE ARE
> NOT TRYING TO BECOME SAINTS;
> WE ARE SAINTS WHO ARE
> BECOMING LIKE CHRIST.

The status of saint is parallel to the concept of being God's called or elect. By the calling or election of God, believers are set apart and from that point forward belong to the sphere of His holiness. We begin our walk with God as immature babes in Christ, but we are indeed children of God. We are saints who sin, but we have all the resources in Christ that we need in order to reject sin. Paul's words to the Ephesians are an interesting combination of these two concepts of holiness. After addressing them as "saints" or holy ones in 1:1 he goes on in verse 4 to declare that God "chose us in Him [Christ] . . . that we should be holy and blameless before Him." By God's choosing, they were already holy in Christ, but the purpose was that they would mature in their character as they conform to the image of God.

As believers, we are not trying to become saints; we are saints who are becoming like Christ. In no way does this deny our continuous struggle with sin, but it does give us hope for the future. Many Christians are dominated by the flesh and deceived by the devil. But telling Christians they are sinners and then disciplining them if they do not act like saints seems counterproductive at best and inconsistent with the Bible at worst.

WHAT IS TRUE

Since we become saints in Christ by God's calling, we share in Christ's inheritance.

> The Spirit Himself bears witness with our Spirit that we are children of God, and if children, heirs also, heirs of God and fellow heirs with Christ (Rom. 8:16-17).

Every believer is identified with Christ:

1. In His death   see Rom. 6:3,6; Gal. 2:20; Col. 3:1-3
2. In His burial   see Rom. 6:4
3. In His resurrection   see Rom. 6:5,8,11
4. In His ascension   see Eph. 2:6
5. In His life   see Rom. 6:10-11
6. In His power   see Eph. 1:19-20
7. In His inheritance   see Rom. 8:16-17; Eph. 1:11-12

The list below itemizes in first-person language who we really are in Christ. These are some of the scriptural traits that reflect who each of us became when we were born again. We cannot earn them or buy them anymore than people born in America can earn or buy the rights and freedoms of American citizens. These rights are guaranteed by the Constitution for all those who are born in the United States. Similarly, the right to be a child of God is guaranteed to us by the Word of God simply because we were born into God's holy family by faith in Christ.

WHO AM I?

I am the salt of the earth (see Matt. 5:13).

I am the light of the world (see Matt. 5:14).

I am a child of God (see John 1:12).

I am part of the true vine, a channel of Christ's life (see John 15:1,5).

I am Christ's friend (see John 15:15).

I am chosen and appointed by Christ to bear His fruit (see John 15:16).

I am a slave of righteousness (see Rom. 6:18).

I am enslaved to God (see Rom. 6:22).

I am a son of God; God is spiritually my Father (see Rom. 8:14-15; Gal. 3:26; 4:6).

I am a joint heir with Christ (see Rom. 8:17).

I am a temple of God. His Spirit dwells in me (see 1 Cor. 3:16; 6:19).

I am united to the Lord and am one spirit with Him (see 1 Cor. 6:17).

I am a member of Christ's Body (see 1 Cor. 12:27; Eph. 5:30).

I am a new creation (see 2 Cor. 5:17).

I am reconciled to God and am a minister of reconciliation (see 2 Cor. 5:18-19).

I am a son of God and one in Christ (see Gal. 3:26,28).

I am an heir of God since I am a son of God (see Gal. 4:6-7).

I am a saint (see Eph. 1:1; 1 Cor. 1:2; Phil. 1:1; Col. 1:2).

I am God's workmanship born anew in Christ to do His work (see Eph. 2:10).

I am a fellow citizen with the rest of God's family (see Eph. 2:19).

I am a prisoner of Christ (see Eph. 3:1; 4:1).

I am righteous and holy (see Eph. 4:24).

I am a citizen of heaven, seated in heaven right now (see Phil. 3:20; Eph. 2:6).

I am hidden with Christ in God (see Col. 3:3).

I am an expression of the life of Christ because He is my life (see Col. 3:4).

I am chosen of God, holy and dearly loved (see Col. 3:12; 1 Thess. 1:4).

I am a son of light and not of darkness (see 1 Thess. 5:5).

I am a holy partaker of a heavenly calling (see Heb. 3:1).

I am a partaker of Christ; I share in His life (see Heb. 3:14).

I am one of God's living stones, being built up in Christ (see 1 Pet. 2:5).

I am a member of a chosen race, a royal priesthood, a holy nation, a people for God's own possession (see 1 Pet. 2:9-10).

I am an alien and stranger to this world in which I temporarily live (see 1 Pet. 2:11).

I am an enemy of the devil (see 1 Pet. 5:8).

I am a child of God and I will resemble Christ when He returns (see 1 John 3:1-2).

I am born of God, and the evil one cannot touch me (see 1 John 5:18).

I am *not* the great "I AM" (see Exod. 3:14; John 8:24, 28,58), but by the grace of God, I am what I am (see 1 Cor. 15:10).

WHO YOU ARE

If you are a born-again child of God, every one of the above verses is true of you, and there is nothing you can do to make them more true or less true. Your self-image will improve, and consequently, your behavior will improve if you make a conscious choice to believe what God has said about you. You will not be prideful if you do, but you may be defeated if you do not. One of the greatest ways to help yourself grow in Christ is to remind yourself continually who you are in Him. I suggest that you go back and read the list aloud right now. Read the list once or twice a day for a week or two. Read it when you think that Satan is trying to deceive you into believing you are a worthless failure.

The more you reaffirm who you are in Christ, the more your behavior will begin to reflect your true identity. Commenting on Romans 6, British writer and church leader John Stott said that the "necessity of remembering who we are [is the way] Paul brings his high theology down to the level of practical everyday experience."[3] Stott writes:

> So, in practice we should constantly be reminding ourselves who we are. We need to learn to talk to ourselves, and ask ourselves questions: "Don't you know? Don't you know the meaning of your conversion and baptism? Don't you know that you have been united to Christ in His death and resurrection? Don't you know that you have been enslaved to God and have committed yourself to His obedience? Don't you know these things? Don't you know who you are?" We must go on pressing ourselves with such questions, until we reply to ourselves: "Yes, I do know who I am, a new person in Christ, and by the grace of God I shall live accordingly."[4]

One man drove several hundred miles to attend our Living Free in Christ conference. On his way home he decided to use the Who Am I? statements as a personal prayer list. As he drove he prayed through the list of traits one by one, asking God to burn them into his subconsciousness. He was on the road for nearly five hours, and he prayed through the Who Am I? verses all the way! When asked about the impact of this experience on his life, with a smile, he simply replied, "Life changing."

One of my students, who sat through this material in a seminary class, was struggling with his identity in Christ. After the class, he sent me this note:

Dear Dr. Anderson:

In looking back over the material presented in class this semester, I realize that I have been freed and enlightened in many ways. I believe the most significant material for me had to do with the fact that in Christ I am significant, accepted and secure. As I meditated on this material, I found that I was able to overcome many problems I have struggled with for years—fear of failure, feelings of worthlessness and a general sense of inadequacy.

I began prayerfully studying the Who Am I? statements given in class. I found myself going back to that list many times during the semester, especially when I felt attacked in the area of fear or inadequacy. I have also been able to share this material with a class at church, and many of my students have experienced new freedom in their lives as well. I can't speak enthusiastically enough about helping people understand who they really are in Christ. In my future ministry I intend to make this a dominant part of my teaching and counseling.

GOING DEEPER

1. What has enslaved you?
2. What is the definition of "sinner"? Of "saint"?
3. How does every believer identify with Christ?
4. How can reading the Who Am I? passages help you be affirmed in your new identity and faith?

CHAPTER 6

SEE YOURSELF FOR WHO YOU REALLY ARE

To make a saint it must indeed be by grace; and whoever doubts this does not know what a saint is, or a man.

BLAISE PASCAL

To become Christlike is the only thing in the whole world worth caring for, the thing before which every ambition of man is folly and all lower achievement vain.

HENRY DRUMMOND

Claire attended a church college ministry I was involved in several years ago. In our physical and material world system,

Claire had very little going for her. She had less-than-average looks. Her father was a hopeless alcoholic who had deserted his family. Her mother worked two menial jobs just to make ends meet. Her older brother, a drug addict, was in and out of the house.

When I first met Claire, she appeared to be the ultimate wallflower. I wondered how she would be received in our college-aged culture, which is enamored by physical beauty and material success. To my pleasant surprise, everybody in the group liked her and loved to be around her. She had lots of friends, and eventually she married the nicest guy in the college department.

What was her secret? Claire simply accepted herself for who God said she was, and she confidently committed herself to God's great goal for her life: to love people and grow in Christ. She was not a threat to anyone. Instead, she was so positive and caring toward others that everyone loved her.

Long before Freedom in Christ existed as a ministry, I had a growing sense that most believers do not really know who they are in Christ. So I organized a one-day spiritual identity conference. I did it as much for my own understanding as I did for those who attended. I was overwhelmed by the response. One of my seminary students attended and came to see me the next week.

Derek grew up with a well-meaning father who demanded perfection from his children. He was an intelligent, talented young man; but no matter how hard he tried or how well he performed, it was never quite good enough. Driven by his father, Derek earned an appointment to the United States Naval Academy in Annapolis, Maryland, and qualified for flight school. He achieved what most young men only dream about: becoming a member of the elite corps of navy fliers. Here is the beginning of Derek's story in his own words:

After I completed my obligation to the Navy, I decided that I wanted to please God with my life. But I saw God as a perfectionistic heavenly shadow of my earthly father. I figured the only way I could fulfill His expectations was to become a missionary. I'll be honest with you. I enrolled in the missions program for the same reason I went to Annapolis: to please a demanding Father.

Then I attended your conference last Saturday. I had never heard that I am unconditionally loved and accepted by my heavenly Father, and I never understood who I already am in Christ. I've always worked hard to gain His acceptance by what I do, just as I struggled to gain the acceptance of my natural father. I didn't realize that I already please Him by who I am in Christ. Now I know that I don't have to be a missionary to please God, so I'm changing my major to practical theology.

Derek studied for a practical theology degree for about a year. Then he had the opportunity to serve on a short-term missionary team in Spain. When Derek returned from his trip, he

WE MUST RECOGNIZE
THE NECESSITY OF BEING
BEFORE DOING, MATURITY
BEFORE MINISTRY AND
CHARACTER BEFORE CAREER.

burst into my office and excitedly told me about his ministry experience in Spain. "I'm changing my major again," he said.

"You're changing back to missions, right?" I responded with a smile.

"Right," Derek beamed. "But I'm not going into missions because I need God's approval. I know God already loves and accepts me as His child. Now I'm planning to be a missionary because I love Him and want to serve Him."

That is the fundamental difference between being driven, which is a prescription for disaster, and being called, which is the basis for our Christian service.

BEING BEFORE DOING

In order to live out our calling, we must recognize the necessity of being before doing, maturity before ministry and character before career. Civilizations have been destroyed when the order is reversed. The same predictable results happen in our churches when leaders lack the character and maturity to lead. The doing got ahead of the being as it did for this pastor:

> I have been reading your two books *Victory over the Darkness* and *The Bondage Breaker*, and I want to thank you for giving two tools that I really needed. I'm the founding pastor of this church having begun 16 years ago and find myself in the first steps of recovering from a church split. I have never known pain like this, Neil, but I am finding it a tremendous time of learning and growth in the Lord. Your Victory book has been especially helpful in that I have tried to find too much of my identity in what I do as a pastor and not enough in who I am as a saint.

The greatest determinant of our success in ministry is our own personal identity and security in Christ. One of the most gifted, talented, personable and intelligent students I have ever taught was in ministry for two years and bombed out. He attended our Living Free in Christ conference and later wrote me this letter:

> I've always figured I was a rotten, no good, dirty, stinking sinner saved by grace yet failing God miserably every day. All I could look forward to was a lifetime of apologizing every night for not being the man I know He wants me to be: "But I will try harder tomorrow Lord." As a firstborn, trying so hard to earn the approval of highly expectant parents, I've related to God the same way. He just couldn't possibly love me as much as He does other "better" believers. Oh sure, I'm saved by grace through faith, but really I'm just hanging on until He gets tired of putting up with me here and brings me home finally to stop the failure in progress. Whew, what a treadmill.
>
> Neil, when you said, "You're not a sinner, you're a saint," in reference to our new, primary identification, you totally blew me away! Isn't that strange that a guy could go clear through a good seminary and never really latch on to the truth that he is, indeed, a new creation in Christ?! I'm convinced that old tapes, laid down in early childhood, can truly hinder our progress in understanding who we are in Christ.
>
> It has been so helpful and liberating to me. I'm beginning to grow out of my old ways of thinking about myself (extremely poor, denigrating self-talk) and about God. I don't constantly picture Him as disappointed in me anymore. If He can still love me and be active in me and find use for me after I failed Him as badly as I did, surely my worth to Him cannot be based on my performance!

He just plain and simply loves me—period. What a new, joyful walk I'm experiencing with Him, praise God.

I have been so deeply touched by these insights, I am taking our people through a study of Ephesians, learning who we are *in Christ* and what we have as believers *in Christ*. My preaching is different, and our people are profiting greatly, being built up in strength and confidence. I can't tell you how gracious the Lord has been to me, Neil, allowing me to try again. Each day of service is a direct gift from God, and I bank each one carefully in heaven's vault for all eternity, to the honor of my Savior.

Committed Christians want to know how to live the Christian life. They want to know how to be a good mother or father, how to help others, how to pray, how to witness, how to do the right thing. Wanting to know how to behave, we turn to our concordances, which direct us to some Old Testament passages and the

> BY SUBMITTING TO GOD
> AND RESISTING THE DEVIL,
> WE FIND OUR IDENTITY AND
> FREEDOM IN CHRIST.

second half of Paul's epistles. Paul's writings can be divided into two halves. The first half is doctrinal. The second half gives practical instruction for living the Christian life. If we are only interested in how we ought to behave, we skip the doctrinal first half and refer to the practical second half. The problem is, the first half establishes us in Christ. If we understand and believe the first half, we will naturally (actually, supernaturally) live out the second half.

This principle works in Christian marriages and families, too. There are more books, radio shows, audiocassettes and degreed programs to help our struggling families than ever. How are we doing? I am sure these tools represent some very sound Christian counsel on parenting, communication and other practical aspects of living out our roles in life. If you are torn up on the inside and do not have a clue as to who you are in Christ, such advice will probably go right over your head. You may try to follow the suggestions for a couple of days, but you will be back where you started: failing to do exactly what Scripture tells you to do. You will still have unanswered questions and be torn up inside when you try to live the Christian life in your own strength and rely solely upon human resources.

Many people cannot even receive the full counsel of God. Paul wrote, "I gave you milk to drink, not solid food; for you were not yet able to receive it. Indeed, even now you are not yet able, for you are still fleshly. For since there is jealousy and strife among you, are you not fleshly, and are you not walking like mere men?" (1 Cor. 3:2-3). Apparently, we would have to help people resolve their jealousies and strife if they are ever going to be able to receive the Word of God. This has proven true in our experience. We have had the privilege to help thousands of people resolve their personal and spiritual conflicts through genuine repentance. By submitting to God and resisting the devil, they find their identity and freedom in Christ. Now they sense the Holy Spirit bearing witness with their spirit that they are children of God (see Rom. 8:16). Suddenly the Bible is understandable, and they begin to grow again.

GETTING A GRIP ON GOD'S GRACE

The importance of knowing who we are in the midst of difficult experiences was brought home to me through the life of a very special young girl named Myndee Hudson. Myndee was a junior high

school girl with long, beautiful blonde hair. I met her when I was
speaking at a camp in Montana. She was unable to attend some of
my talks and later apologized for her absence, saying she was sick.
It turned out that Myndee was deathly sick. Two days after
camp Myndee was rushed to Denver, Colorado, for delicate
emergency surgery to remove a malignant tumor invading her
brain stem and spinal cord. The surgery lasted 12 hours. During
recovery, she developed pneumonia. Doctors offered little hope
that she would make it to the end of the year.

Myndee was a believer and a fighter. She found a passage of
Scripture to guide her through her battles. Romans 8:35,37-38
seemed to be written just for her:

> Who shall separate us from the love of Christ? Shall
> trouble or hardship or persecution or famine or naked-
> ness or danger or sword? No, in all these things we are
> more than conquerors through him who loved us. For
> I am convinced that neither death nor life, neither angels
> nor demons, neither the present nor the future, nor any
> powers, neither height nor depth, nor anything else in all
> creation, will be able to separate us from the love of God
> that is in Christ Jesus our Lord (*NIV*).

Myndee held on to that truth, because it was more than words
to her. She recovered from surgery and pneumonia and started
chemotherapy. Then she had radiation treatment, which made
her sick, and she lost most of her hair.

When I visited Myndee in her home, she met me at the door
wearing a blonde wig. She had lost more than 20 pounds. Her
voice was raspy from the radiation treatments, and she looked
very weak.

"How are you doing, Myndee?" I asked, fighting back my
tears.

Myndee broke through the pain and awkward silence by saying, "Do you want to see my wig?" Before I could respond she
pulled the wig off her head and thrust it toward me. Her beautiful, long blonde hair was gone except for small patches that
draped from her head like thin strands of ribbon.

This was no vain girl devastated by the loss of her physical
beauty. This was a child of God who had found a greater beauty
inside because of her relationship with her heavenly Father.

"Dave, I wish every kid could have cancer," Myndee said.

I could not hide the look of shock. "Myndee, why do you say
that?"

She smiled cutely and said, "Because then they would realize
what's really important in life. The only things my friends seem
to care about are things that don't last: boyfriends, what your
hair looks like, who likes you. It's all so unimportant compared
to knowing God. I used to be that way, too."

She paused for a moment, and then she smiled at me and
continued. "When you know you're going to die, you only care
about the things that are going to last. Before I was sick, Jesus
was only a part of my life. Now He's everything to me."

Would that all God's children be that mature. Myndee
Hudson died before she got out of junior high school. But she
learned more and affected more lives for Christ than many
Christians who live decades longer. She had learned to "seek first
His kingdom and His righteousness" (Matt. 6:33).

RECOGNIZING OUR SANCTIFICATION IN CHRIST

Are you aware that salvation for the believer is past, present and
future tense? By that we mean, we have been saved (past tense,
see Eph. 2:4-5,8), we are being saved (present tense, see 1 Cor.
1:18; 2 Cor. 2:15) and someday we will be fully saved from the

wrath that is to come (future tense, see Rom. 5:9-10; 13:11). We have not yet experienced the totality of salvation, but we believe that we can have the assurance of it. Paul wrote, "You were sealed in Him with the Holy Spirit of promise, who is given as a pledge of our inheritance, with a view to the redemption of God's own possession, to the praise of His glory" (Eph. 1:13-14). John wrote, "These things I have written to you who believe in the name of the Son of God, so that you may know that you have eternal life" (1 John 5:13).

In reference to the believer, sanctification is also past, present and future tense. We have been sanctified (past tense, see 2 Pet. 1:3-4; 1 Cor. 6:19), we are being sanctified (present tense, see Rom. 6:22; 2 Cor. 7:1), and we shall some day be fully sanctified (future tense, see 1 Thess. 3:12-13; 5:23-24). The doctrine of sanctification begins at our new birth and ends in our glorification. Past tense sanctification is usually referred to as positional sanctification and refers to the position or the status the believer has in Christ. Present tense sanctification is referred to as progressive or experiential sanctification.

The positional truth of who we are in Christ is real truth, and it is the basis for our progressive sanctification. Just as the past reality of salvation is the basis for the present tense working out of our salvation, so also is our position in Christ the basis for our growth in Christ. In other words, believers are not trying to become children of God; we are already children of God who are becoming like Christ.

Overemphasizing positional sanctification can lead to a denial of sin. One man understood only positional sanctification and thought it was a done deal. He said, "I haven't sinned in 20 years." I asked him if his wife would agree with that.

If we say that we have no sin, we are deceiving ourselves, and the truth is not in us (1 John 1:8).

It comes back to understanding that having sin and being a sinner are separate issues.

On the other hand, people who overemphasize progressive sanctification at the expense of positional sanctification spend the rest of their lives trying to become somebody they already are. Their tendency is to say, "That is just positional truth," as though it is not real truth.

BEING RIGHT WITH GOD

A few years ago a pastor asked me to counsel a couple from his church. I have never seen a couple so blown apart in my life. As they entered my office, they were attacking each other and ready to separate. I prayed silently to the Lord, *If there's any way of saving this marriage, You're the only one who knows about it.*

After several minutes of listening to this couple bitterly complain about each other, I interrupted and said to the wife, "Is there a way you can get away for a while all by yourself?"

She thought for a moment and nodded. She said, "Our family has a cabin in the hills. I can use that."

I asked if she would be willing to go, and she said she would. So I gave her a set of our conference tapes and asked her to go through them, not to save the marriage, but for her own walk with God. She agreed. I asked the husband—who happened to be a music minister at my friend's church—to listen to a set of the same tapes while his wife was away. As they left my office, I had little hope that I would ever see them together again.

Two years later I was sitting in a restaurant with my wife when that same music minister walked in with his three children. *Oh, no,* I thought, *they've split up for good.* I kind of hoped that he would not see or recognize me. To my surprise and delight, his wife walked into the restaurant after parking the car. They seemed happy to be with each other.

Finally they looked my way and greeted me cheerfully.

"How are you doing?" I asked.

"We're doing great," the wife answered. "I did what you told me to do. I went up into the hills alone for two weeks, listened to your tapes and had an encounter with God."

"I also listened to the tapes and had an encounter with God," the husband added, "after which we were able to work out the problems in our marriage."

This couple discovered that reconciliation between two humans begins by being reconciled with God. They could not experience their oneness in Christ when one or both of them had unresolved issues between themselves and God. There is no true reconciliation without repentance and forgiveness on the part of both parties. God is the only one who did not have to repent in order for there to be reconciliation, but He did have to provide a means to forgive us—which He supplied in Christ. Consequently, when we come to Him in faith, we are reconciled to Him, as Paul explains in Romans 5:8-11:

> But God demonstrates His own love toward us, in that while we were yet sinners, Christ died for us. Much more then, having now been justified by His blood, we shall be saved from the wrath of God through Him. For if while we were enemies, we were reconciled to God through the death of His Son, much more, having been reconciled, we shall be saved by His life. And not only this, but we also exult in God through our Lord Jesus Christ, through whom we have now received the reconciliation.

It is good to know that our sins are forgiven, but that is not enough to experience our victory. We have been given spiritual life and a new identity—we have been reconciled to God. Read the passages below and repeat them aloud until they become a part of you. Occasionally pray through the list, asking God to implant these truths in your heart.

Since I have been reconciled to God in Christ, by the grace of God:

I have been justified—completely forgiven and made righteous (see Rom. 5:1).

I died with Christ and died to the power of sin's rule over my life (see Rom. 6:1-6).

I am free forever from condemnation (see Rom. 8:1).

I have been placed into Christ by God's doing (see 1 Cor. 1:30).

I have received the Spirit of God into my life that I might know the things freely given to me by God (see 1 Cor. 2:12).

I have been given the mind of Christ (see 1 Cor. 2:16).

I have been bought with a price; I am not my own; I belong to God (see 1 Cor. 6:19-20).

I have been established, anointed and sealed by God in Christ, and I have been given the Holy Spirit as a pledge guaranteeing my inheritance to come (see 2 Cor. 1:21; Eph. 1:13-14).

Since I have died, I no longer live for myself but for Christ (see 2 Cor. 5:14-15).

I have been made righteous (see 2 Cor. 5:21).

I have been crucified with Christ, and it is no longer I who live; Christ lives in me. The life I am now living is Christ's life (see Gal. 2:20).

I have been blessed with every spiritual blessing (see Eph. 1:3).

I was chosen in Christ before the foundation of the world to be holy and without blame before Him (see Eph. 1:4).

I was predestined to be adopted as God's son (see Eph. 1:5).

I have been redeemed and forgiven, and I am a recipient of His grace. I have been made alive together with Christ (see Eph. 2:5).

I have been raised up and seated with Christ in heaven (see Eph.
2:6).

I have direct access to God through the Spirit (see Eph. 2:18).

I may approach God with boldness, freedom and confidence (see
Eph. 3:12).

I have been rescued from the domain of Satan's rule and transferred to the kingdom of Christ (see Col. 1:13).

I have been redeemed and forgiven of all my sins. The debt
against me has been canceled (see Col. 1:14).

Christ Himself is in me (see Col. 1:27).

I am firmly rooted in Christ and am now being built in Him (see
Col. 2:7).

I have been spiritually circumcised (see Col. 2:11).

I have been made complete in Christ (see Col. 2:10).

I have been buried, raised and made alive with Christ (see Col.
2:12-13).

I died with Christ and I have been raised up with Christ. My life
is now hidden with Christ in God. Christ is now my life (see
Col. 3:1-4).

I have been given a spirit of power, love and self-discipline (see
2 Tim. 1:7).

I have been saved and set apart according to God's doing (see
2 Tim. 1:9; Titus 3:5).

Because I am sanctified and am one with the Sanctifier, He is not
ashamed to call me brother (see Heb. 2:11).

I have the right to come boldly before the throne of God to find
mercy and grace in time of need (see Heb. 4:16).

I have been given exceedingly great and precious promises by
God by which I am a partaker of God's divine nature (see
2 Pet. 1:4).

Becky was a first-year college student home for break when
she attended a small-group Bible study in my house. We were

studying the battle for the mind and discussing the biblical truths found in another book that Neil wrote, titled *The Bondage Breaker*. One night Becky asked if she could talk with me. "What's on your heart?" I asked. She stood silent for some time; then, with tear-filled eyes, she said, "I don't think anybody loves me!" Becky came from a broken home; her parents divorced when she was very young, but it was obvious that the wound was still festering. The pain in her voice reflected her continual struggle with her family, an eating disorder and a dangerously poor self-image.

"Becky, do you remember the two lists I shared with the group tonight about who we are in Christ?" I asked.

"Yes," she said, still fighting back the tears.

"Do you believe those passages are true of you right now, without changing anything about yourself?" I continued.

"Oh, I don't know," she said. The frustration in her voice was obvious.

"Let me read them to you again. Better yet, why don't you read them to me," I offered.

She agreed and began to read the truth about herself. At first the tone of her voice lacked enthusiasm, but gradually a change occurred. Her voice became more confident and a smile began to appear. By the time she finished the list, she was even laughing.

That is incredible. Did any of Becky's circumstances change as she read the biblical truth about who she is in Christ? No. The only thing that changed was her understanding of who she is in Christ.

Dick Anderson, the past chairman of the board at Freedom in Christ Ministries, shared this story:

A lady in our church dropped by my office for counseling this week. She has been struggling in her relationship with her alcoholic husband. She was at her wit's end, feeling terribly defeated. She came to tell me she was calling it quits on their marriage.

I pulled out the list of passages you have in *Victory over the Darkness*, concerning who we are in Christ. I said, "I would like you to read this aloud." She read about halfway through the list and began to cry. She said, "I never realized all this was true of me. I feel that maybe there is hope for me after all."

GOING DEEPER

1. Why is the idea of *being* before *doing* so important?
2. How have we been sanctified? How are we being sanctified? How will we be sanctified?
3. How does grace reconcile us to God?
4. How does the list of what Christ has done for you change your understanding of yourself?

CHAPTER 7

A NEW HEART
AND A NEW
SPIRIT

The heart has its reasons which reason knows nothing of.

BLAISE PASCAL

*The eyes see what the heart loves. If the heart loves God and is single in this
devotion, then the eyes will see God whether others see Him or not.*

WARREN WIERSBE

One of the most dramatic turnarounds I have witnessed in a person occurred in Jenny. At 23, Jenny was a pretty Christian girl
with a seemingly pleasant personality. She had loving parents

and came from a good church. But she was torn up inside and deeply depressed. She had failed at college and was on the verge of being fired from her job. On top of that, she had suffered from eating disorders for several years.

Jenny claimed to be a Christian, so I challenged her with the biblical truth about who she was in Christ. I was sharing with her the good news of her spiritual identity when she said, "Are you always this positive?"

"It's not a matter of being positive," I answered. "It's a matter of believing the truth. Because of your relationship with God, this is who you are in Christ." She left our meeting with a glimmer of hope.

Several weeks later Jenny attended a one-month spiritual retreat at my invitation. Shortly after we arrived, I sat down with her privately. "I didn't invite you here to change your behavior," I said. "Your behavior isn't your problem."

"I've always been told that my behavior is my problem," she answered, looking a little surprised at my statement. "Everyone I know is trying to change my behavior."

I responded, "I'm not worried about your behavior. It's your beliefs I'm interested in, because what you do is just a product of what you believe. I want to change your beliefs about who God is and who you are as a child of God. You're not a failure. You're not a sick individual who is a problem to your parents and to your church. You are a child of God, no better and no worse than any other person at this retreat. I want you to start believing it, because it's the truth."

MOST PEOPLE'S BELIEFS

Attend any Bible-believing church and ask the congregation, "How many of you believe that you are a sinner?" Almost everyone will raise his or her hand. Then ask, "How many of you believe that you are a saint?" Few, if any, will respond. Why do so many Christians view themselves this way? Because most of us have been taught that that is who we are—it is what I was taught.

Some Christians think it would be prideful to identity themselves as saints. Others believe the label "sinner" best fits their present condition. They sin, so they must be sinners. Even if someone told them they are a combination of saint and sinner, they will believe the latter over the former because it best fits their experience. Most people get their identity and sense of worth from their experience rather than from the Word of God.

My friend and colleague Dr. Robert Saucy, the chairman of the theology department at Talbot School of Theology, submitted a paper to the Evangelical Society concerning our identity in Christ (available on our website, www.ficm.org). When he read the paper identifying Christians as saints, not one in attendance disagreed, because that is clearly what Scripture teaches. If we are just sinners, then what do sinners do, and what does it imply about our core identity?

Being a saint who is alive and free in Christ does not imply spiritual maturity or sinless perfection, but it does provide the basis for hope and future growth. Despite God's provision for us in Christ, we are still far less than perfect. We are saints who sin. Our position in Christ is settled, but personal failure and disobedience often mar our daily performance, disappointing us and disrupting the harmony of our relationship with God. We groan with the apostle Paul, "The good that I wish, I do not do; but I practice the very evil that I do not wish. . . . Wretched man that I am! Who will set me free from the body of this death?" (Rom. 7:19,24).

In our attempts to understand the failure that often disturbs our sense of sainthood, we struggle with such biblical terms as "flesh," "nature" and "old man" (self). What do these terms really mean? Are they distinct in themselves or inter-changeable? Defining these concepts becomes even more diffi-cult when the *New International Version* of the Bible translates "flesh" (*sarx*) as "sinful nature" (see Rom. 7:18; 8:3-5; 1 Cor. 5:5; and others).

Admittedly these can be difficult theological issues. Bible scholars have wrestled with these questions for centuries, and we do not in any way pretend to have the final answers. However, we want to explore some of these terms that often confuse Christians who attempt to deal with the sinful side of sainthood. A biblical grasp of these terms further assists us in understanding who we are and paves the way for greater spiri-tual maturity.[1]

THE NATURE OF THE PROBLEM

The Bible teaches that we were dead in our trespasses and sins (see Eph. 2:1) and "were by *nature* children of wrath" (Eph. 2:3, emphasis added). In other words, we were born physically alive but spiritually dead. We had neither the presence of God in our lives nor the knowledge of His ways. Consequently, we all learned to live our lives independent of God. This learned inde-pendence is one of the chief characteristics of the flesh. "The flesh sets its desire against the Spirit, and the Spirit against the flesh; for these are in opposition to one another" (Gal. 5:17). They are in opposition because the Holy Spirit, like Jesus, will not operate independent of our heavenly Father, but the flesh does. The flesh may be defined as existence apart from God—a life dominated by sin or a drive opposed to God. The flesh is self-reliant rather than God-dependent; it is self-centered rather than Christ-centered.

Such is the state of fallen humanity: sinful by nature and spiritually dead, i.e., separated from God. In addition, the heart which is the center of our being "is more deceitful than all else and is desperately sick" (Jer. 17:9). Paul says, "All have sinned and fall short of the glory of God" (Rom. 3:23). Fallen humanity lives life "in the flesh," and "those who are in the flesh cannot please God" (Rom. 8:8). Humanity was depraved. Every aspect of our beings was corrupted, and there is nothing we can do to save ourselves.

> WE HAVE A CHOICE. WE CAN WALK ACCORDING TO THE FLESH OR WE CAN WALK ACCORDING TO THE SPIRIT.

The question is, What changed at salvation? First, God transferred us from the domain of darkness to the kingdom of His beloved Son (see Col. 1:13). Second, sin's dominion through the flesh was broken. As we explained in chapter 5, as believers, we are no longer in the flesh, but we are in Christ. Paul explains, "However, you are not in the flesh but in the Spirit, if indeed the Spirit of God dwells in you. But if anyone does not have the Spirit of Christ, he does not belong to Him" (Rom. 8:9). Paul also equates the idea of being in the flesh with being in Adam. "For as *in Adam* all die, so also *in Christ* all will be made alive" (1 Cor. 15:22, emphasis added). Christians are no longer in the flesh, but since the characteristics of the flesh remain in believers, we have a choice. We can walk (or live) according to the flesh (see Gal. 5:19-21) or we can walk (or live) according to the Spirit (see Gal. 5:22-23). This positional change can be shown as follows:

In Adam		In Christ
Old man (self)	by ancestry	New man (self)
Sin nature see Eph. 2:1-3	by nature	Partaker of divine nature see 2 Pet. 1:4
In the flesh see Rom. 8:8	by birth	In the Spirit see Rom. 8:9
Live according to the flesh	by choice	Live according to the Spirit or the flesh see Gal. 5:16-18

A good illustration of what has happened to us is found in the Narnia series character Eustace in C. S. Lewis's book *Voyage of the Dawn Treader*. Eustace was a boy who was so awful and nasty that he turned into an ugly, evil dragon. One might make a point about the toughness of his skin and how it correlates with the hardness of a natural man's heart, but we get the idea that the dragon represents the evil and sinfulness of the natural man. Then he encountered the great and powerful lion, Aslan, who represents Christ. Aslan does not just change him back into a boy; Aslan transforms his heart, and the dragon is transfigured into a fine young man.

At first Eustace attempts to bring about his transformation by his own means. Scratching and clawing at his own flesh, he peeled off layer after layer of his dragon skin. But for every layer that came off, another layer of wrinkled, scaly skin appeared underneath. Endless dragon layers means that we humans are totally depraved: We are in a position where we can do nothing to please God, and we possess no holiness to remove or combat sin. Finally, Aslan stepped up to do the job. With one painful swipe of his powerful claws, the lion cut to the heart of Eustace's dragon flesh and peeled it away, and Eustace the boy stepped out.

One moment Eustace was a dragon; the next moment he was a boy. He went from one to the other; he was not part dragon and part boy. Eustace is a picture of what the Bible proclaims about us. Once we were in the kingdom of Satan; now we are in the kingdom of God. Once we were in the flesh; now we are in the Spirit. "For you were formerly darkness, but now you are light in the Lord; walk as children of light" (Eph. 5:8).

THE NEED TO BE GRAFTED IN

In Arizona, city parks and boulevards are decorated with ornamental orange trees which are a much hardier stock than the trees which produce the sweet oranges we eat. Because these trees can survive colder temperatures, they are used for what is called rootstock.

The ornamental orange is allowed to grow to a certain height; then it is cut off, and a new life (such as a navel orange) is grafted in. Everything that grows above the graft takes on the new nature of the sweet orange. Everything below the graft retains the physical characteristics of the ornamental orange. There is only one tree when it is fully grown. The *physical* growth of the tree is still dependent upon the roots that go deep into the soil for water and nutrition. What grows above the graft takes on only the nature of the navel orange.

Nobody looks at a grove of navel oranges and says, "That grove is nothing more than a bunch of rootstock!" People call them navel orange trees because they identify the trees by their fruit. The same applies for us. Jesus said, "So then, you will know them by their fruits" (Matt. 7:20). Paul added, "Therefore from now on we recognize no man according to the flesh" (2 Cor. 5:16). In other words, we are not supposed to recognize Christians for who we were in Adam, but for who we now are in Christ. That is why the Bible does not identify believers as sinners, but instead, we are identified as saints.

The natural person is like an ornamental orange tree: he or she may look good but he or she can only bear bitter fruit. (The fruit will only drop to the ground and bring forth more natural stock that will only appear to look good for a season.)

What is the nature of the tree? Would it have two natures? It depends upon whether we refer to the whole tree, which does have two natures (rootstock and navel), or we only focus on the part of the tree which grows above the graft (the new creation), which has just one nature (navel). Whether Christians have one or two natures is somewhat of a semantic problem. When Paul describes the new person in Christ (new nature), he differentiates between who we are in Christ and who we were in the flesh (old nature). Paul wrote, "Now those who belong to Christ Jesus have crucified the flesh with its passions and desires" (Gal. 5:24). The flesh no longer describes who we are, and it is our responsibility to render it inoperative.

In horticulture, we also know that suckers can grow out of roots. They have to be cut off or they will impede the growth of the tree above the graft. This provides a lesson we can apply to our lives. Time and energy spent living by the flesh, just like suckers, is time not spent living by the Spirit, which produces real fruit. Jesus said, "Every branch in Me that does not bear fruit, He takes away; and every branch that bears fruit, He prunes it, that it may bear more fruit" (John 15:2).

Spiritual growth in the Christian life requires a relationship with God, who is our fountain. This relationship will bring forth a new seed of life. Unless there is some seed of life within an organism, growth cannot take place. Likewise, unless there is a root of life within the believer—i.e., some core of spiritual life—growth is impossible. There is nothing to grow. That is why Paul's theology is based upon our position in Christ. "As you therefore have received Christ Jesus the Lord, so walk *in Him*, having been firmly rooted and now being built up *in Him*" (Col. 2:6-7, emphasis added). In order to build up believers (progressive sanctification), we must first be firmly rooted in Christ (positional sanctification).

A NEW HEART

According to Scripture, the center of a person is the heart. It is the "wellspring of life" (Prov. 4:23, *NIV*). In our natural state, "The heart is deceitful above all things and beyond cure" (Jer. 17:9, *NIV*). It is deceitful because it has been conditioned from the time of birth by the deception of a fallen world rather than by the truth of God's Word.

One of the greatest prophesies concerning our salvation is given in Ezekiel 36:26: "I will give you a new heart and put a new spirit within you; I will remove from you your heart of stone and give you a heart of flesh" (*NIV*). According to the new covenant in which every Christian lives under, God promises, "I will put my laws upon their heart" (Heb. 10:16). In other words, "To all the ornamental oranges that will choose to put their trust in God and believe His word, you shall be navel oranges." The moment we were grafted into the vine we were sanctified or set apart as a child of God. We are already clean (see John 15:3), and we can continue to be sanctified as He prunes us so that we may grow and bear fruit.

The same idea is captured in Paul's testimony: "I have been crucified with Christ and I no longer live, but Christ lives in me. The life I live in the body, I live by faith in the Son of God, who loved me and gave himself for me" (Gal. 2:20, *NIV*). Paul says he died, but he lives, obviously a new and different person (see Col. 3:1-3).

A New Person

Parallel to the concept of being a new creation in Christ is the teaching that the believer has put on the "new self" (Col. 3:10) or, more precisely the new man. The new man at times refers both to the new individual (i.e., self) in Christ and to the new humanity or the humanity of the new creation, united in Christ as its head. F. F. Bruce says, "The new man who is created is the new personality that each believer becomes when he is reborn as a member of the new creation whose source of life is Christ."[2]

What does it mean to be a new man? Does it mean that every aspect of the believer is new in reality? We still look the same physically, and we still have many of the same thoughts, feelings and experiences. Compare this to a picture of an ornamental orange tree that has just had a tiny new stem grafted into it. Because so much appears to be the same when we become believers, it is thought by some that our newness refers only to our position in Christ. There is no real change in us until we are finally transformed in glorification. But that would be like teaching justification without regeneration (i.e., we are forgiven, but there is no new life). If we are still ornamental orange trees, how can we be expected to bear navel oranges? We have to believe that our new identity is in the life of Christ and commit ourselves to grow accordingly.

When I was in the navy, we called the captain of our ship the Old Man. My first Old Man was a bad person, and nobody liked him. He drank with the chiefs, belittled his junior officers and made life miserable for the rest of us. He was a lousy Old Man. But if I was going to survive on board that ship, I had to do so under his authority, relating to him as my Old Man. Then one day he got transferred to another ship. I no longer had any relationship with him, and I was no longer under his authority.

We got a new skipper who was very different. How do you think I related to the new Old Man? At first I responded to him just like I had been conditioned to respond to the old Old Man. As I got to know the new skipper, I realized that he was a good man. But I had been programmed for two years to react a certain way when I saw a captain's braids. I did not need to react that way any longer, but it took several months to recondition myself.

When we were dead in our trespasses and sins, we also served under a cruel self-serving master. The admiral of that fleet was Satan, the prince of darkness, the god and ruler of this world. By God's grace, we have been delivered from servitude to him to servitude to Christ. We serve the Lord Jesus Christ, and our new self is infused with the divine nature of Jesus Christ, who is the only five-star admiral in the universe. As children of God, we are no longer under the authority of Satan, nor are we dominated by sin and death. The old man is dead.

NEW THINGS

Despite the fact that every believer will choose at times to live according to the flesh, as did Paul, we are new persons. We are new in relationship to God and new in ourselves.

The change that takes place in us when we come to Christ involves two dimensions. First, we have a new master. As mortals we have no choice but to live under a spiritual power, either our heavenly Father or the god of this world. At salvation, believers in Christ experience a change in the power that dominates their lives. Second, there is an actual change in the nature of the believer, causing the propensities of his or her life or the deepest desires of his or her heart to be oriented toward God rather than toward self and sin.

This becomes evident when a believer chooses to sin. We come under conviction. What we are doing is no longer consistent with who we really are in Christ. I have counseled hundreds of Christians who are questioning their salvation because of their struggle with sin. The fact that sin even bothers them is the best argument for their salvation. If they were not true Christians, the sin with which they struggle would not even bother them. On the other hand, it is the nature of a natural person to sin. There are people who profess to be Christians but have little or no remorse for sin. I would question their salvation. If we are children of God, we are not going to live comfortably with sin.

Why do we need the nature of Christ within us? So we can *be* like Christ, not just *act* like Him. God has not given us the power to imitate Him. He has made us partakers of His nature (see 2 Pet. 1:4) so that we can actually *be* like Him. No one becomes a Christian by acting like one. We are not on a performance basis with God. Under the New Covenant, He does not say, "Here are my standards; now you measure up." He knows we cannot solve the problem of an old sinful self simply by improving our behavior. He must change our core nature by giving us an entirely new self (the life of Christ in us), which is the grace we need to live righteous lives.

Jesus made this point in His Sermon on the Mount: "Unless your righteousness surpasses that of the scribes and Pharisees, you shall not enter the kingdom of heaven" (Matt. 5:20). The scribes and Pharisees were the religious perfectionists of their day. They had external behavior down to a science, but their hearts were like the inside of a tomb: reeking of death. Jesus came to create new persons from the inside out by infusing in them a new nature and creating in them a new self. Only after we become partakers of His divine nature can we live righteous lives.

A New Master

Since we are identified with Christ in His death and resurrection, we have become new persons and part of the new humanity.

In this change we have come under a new power of dominion in our lives. This is clearly expressed in Romans 6:5-7:

> If we have been united with him . . . in his death, we will certainly also be united with him in his resurrection. For we know that our old self [old man] was crucified with him so that the body of sin might be done away with, that we should no longer be slaves to sin—because anyone who has died has been freed from sin (*NIV*).

The old man in relation to believers has been crucified in Christ and they have put on the new man (see Col. 3:10).

Paul adds to our understanding: "Even so consider yourselves to be dead to sin, but alive to God in Christ Jesus" (Rom. 6:11). We do not consider it so in order to make it so. We are to believe continually that we are alive in Christ and dead to sin, *because it is so*. Believing something does not make it true. God said it is true, therefore we believe it. Death is the ending of a relationship, not existence. Sin is still present, appealing and powerful. But when any one of us is tempted to sin, we can say, "I don't have to do that. By the grace of God I can live a righteous life."

Romans 8:1-2 illustrates the point: "There is therefore now no condemnation for those who are in Christ Jesus. For the law of the Spirit of life in Christ Jesus has set you free from the law of sin and of death." Is the law of sin and of death still operative? Yes, that is why Paul calls it a law. We cannot do away with a law, but we can overcome this one by a greater law, which is the law of life in Christ Jesus.

As mortals we cannot fly in our own strength, but we can fly in an airplane, because an airplane has a power greater than the law of gravity. If anyone thinks the law of gravity no longer affects us, they can put their theory to a test by flipping the switch off at 30,000 feet. They will crash and burn.

If we walk by faith according to what God says is true in the power of the Holy Spirit, we will not carry out "the desires of the flesh" (Gal. 5:16). If we believe a lie and live according to the flesh, we too will crash and burn.

SAVED AND SANCTIFIED

Paul writes, "Our old self was crucified" (past tense). We try and try to put the old man to death, but we cannot do it. Why? Because he is already dead. A dear pastor who heard of our ministry asked for an appointment. He said, "I have struggled for 22 years in ministry, and I finally think I know what the answer is. In my devotions I read the following passage, 'For you have died and your life is hidden with Christ in God' (Col. 3:3). That's it, isn't it?" When I assured him it was, he asked, "How do I do that?" I suggested that he read the passage just a little more slowly. For 22 years this man had been desperately trying to become somebody he already was—just like so many other believers. We cannot do for ourselves what Christ has already accomplished for us.

Many Christians struggling with a negative self-image are victims of the Galatians heresy. Paul wrote in Galatians 3:2-3, "I would like to learn just one thing from you: Did you receive the Spirit by observing the law, or by believing what you heard? Are you so foolish? After beginning with the Spirit, are you now trying to attain your goal by human effort?" (*NIV*). We are saved by faith, and we walk or live by faith. We have been justified by faith, and we are being sanctified by faith alone. We are neither saved nor sanctified by how we behave, but by how we believe.

As we have shown throughout this book, God's work of atonement changes sinners to saints. The radical change, called regeneration, is effected at the moment of salvation. The ongoing change in the believer's daily walk continues throughout his or her life. This is so important that we repeat it again: The progressive work of sanctification is only fully effective when the radical, inner transformation by regeneration is realized and appropriated by faith.

THE INDICATIVE AND THE IMPERATIVE

The greatest tension in the New Testament is between the indicative (what God has already done and what is already true about us) and the imperative (what remains to be done as we respond to God by faith and obedience in the power of the Holy Spirit). We must know and believe positional truth if we want to successfully progress in our sanctification. If we do not embrace this fundamental truth, we will keep trying to do for ourselves what God has already done for us. The balance between the indicative and the imperative is about equal in Scripture, but we have not observed that in our churches. Most of the teaching

> WE NEED TO WORSHIP GOD FOR ALL HE HAS DONE AND REST IN THE FINISHED WORK OF CHRIST.

that we have heard focuses on the imperatives. A person could go to some churches for years and never hear or understand that they are children of God who are alive and free in Christ. We need to worship God for all He has done and rest in the finished work of Christ. We need to hear repeatedly the wonderful identity and position we already have in Christ, and then we will be better prepared to receive further instructions and assume our responsibility for living Christian lives.

A Diamond

As a new Christian, each of us was like a lump of coal: unattractive, somewhat fragile and messy. With time and pressure, however, coal becomes hardened and beautiful. Even though the original lump of coal is not fully developed as a diamond, it consists of the right substance to become one. Right now you may be a diamond in the rough, but given enough time and pressure, you can be like a diamond that reveals the glory of God. Anthony Hoekema comments, "You are new creatures now! Not totally new, to be sure, but genuinely new. And we who are believers should see ourselves in this way: no longer as depraved and helpless slaves of sin, but as those who have been created anew in Christ Jesus."[3]

Going Deeper

1. What is the difference between a sinner and a saint? Are you a sinner or a saint?
2. What do we inherit from Adam, and what do we inherit from Christ?
3. What does to be grafted in mean?
4. How do we take off the old man and put on the new man?

CHAPTER 8

LESSONS IN GRACE

Grace freely justifies me and sets me free from the slavery of sin.

BERNARD OF CLAIRVAUX

Neither in heaven nor on Earth is it possible just to settle down comfortably through grace and do nothing and care for nobody else. If I am saved by grace, then I am a worker through grace. If I am justified by grace, then through grace I am a worker for justice. If through grace I am placed within the truth, then through grace I am a servant of truth. If through grace I have been placed within peace, then through grace I am a servant of peace for all men.

CHRISTOPH BLUMHARDT

The sign on the door read, Puppies for Sale. So the little boy went inside to look. The man inside the pet store showed him five little puppies that were ready to leave their mother. They were about the cutest dogs the little boy had ever seen.

"How much are they?" the little boy asked.

The man replied, "Some are 50 dollars, some are more."

The little boy reached in his pocket and pulled out some change. After counting it, he said, "I have a dollar and 47 cents."

"Well, I'm afraid I can't sell you one of these puppies for just a dollar and 47 cents, little boy. You'll have to save your money and come back next time we have more puppies for sale."

About that time, the pet-store owner's wife brought out another puppy that had been hidden in the back of the store. It was smaller than the other puppies and had a bad leg. It could not stand up very well, and when it tried to walk, it limped very badly.

"What's wrong with that puppy?" asked the little boy. The pet-store owner explained that the veterinarian had examined the puppy and had discovered that it did not have a hip socket. It would always limp and always be lame.

"Oh, I wish I had the money to buy that puppy," the little boy exclaimed with excitement. "That is the puppy I would choose!"

"Well that puppy is not for sale, son. But if you really want him, I'll just give him to you. No charge," the owner offered.

The little boy became quite upset at this. He looked straight at the pet-store owner and said, "No, I don't want you to give him to me. That little dog is worth every bit as much as the other dogs you have for sale. I'll give you a dollar and 47 cents now, and I'll give you 50 cents a month until I have paid for this dog in full."

The pet-store owner was perplexed. He said, "You don't really want to spend your money on this little dog, son. He is never going to be able to run and play with you like other puppies."

Then the little boy reached down and pulled up his pant leg to reveal a twisted, crippled left leg, supported by a metal brace.

He looked up at the pet-store owner and said, "Mister, I don't run and play too good myself. I figure this little puppy is going to need someone like me who understands."[1]

UNDERSTANDING GOD'S FAVOR

Grace is unwarranted favor. It cannot be earned, and it is not deserved. Salvation is a free gift and we owe God nothing for it. But a strange thing happens when we receive His grace. We discover that it is more blessed to give than to receive, and those who know it give it away. That is why it is important to know the full gospel and all that we have received in Christ. Those who know who they are in Christ freely give as they have freely received. "We love, because He first loved us" (1 John 4:19). We are to be merciful as He has been merciful to us (see Luke 6:36), and we are to forgive as Jesus has forgiven us (see Eph. 4:32).

> Every good thing bestowed and every perfect gift is from above, coming down from the Father of lights, with whom there is no variation, or shifting shadow (Jas. 1:17).

One reason some people struggle with their spiritual heritage is their uncertainty about what defines a relationship. Let me illustrate. When I was born physically, I had a father. His name was Marvin Anderson. He and I are blood related.

Is there anything that I could possibly do which would change my blood relationship to my father? What if I ran away from home and changed my name? I would still be Marvin Anderson's son. What if he kicked me out of the house? What if he disowned me? Would I still be his son? Of course! We are related by blood and nothing can change that. It is a biological fact.

On the other hand, is there anything I could do that would affect the harmony of our relationship as father and son? Yes, indeed—and by the time I was five years old, I had discovered almost every way! My relationship with my father was never in jeopardy, but my adolescent behavior interrupted the harmony of our relationship countless times.

My father was a taskmaster. When he said run, he meant run. If I walked, it would be best if I kept on walking. Consequently, I learned obedience through the things I suffered, much like someone else did (see Heb. 5:8)! Yes, Christ learned through obedience, too.

The harmony issue was addressed repeatedly as a result of both my good behavior and misbehavior. I discovered that if I obeyed dad, I lived in harmony with him. If I did not obey him, we did not live and work together harmoniously. Whether we lived in harmony or not, he remained my father, because we are blood related.

Then one day I was born again. I became a member of God's family. God is my spiritual Father, and I enjoy an eternal relationship with Him through the precious blood of Jesus Christ (see 1 Pet. 1:18-19). As a child of God, is there anything I can do that will change my relationship with Him? I realize that people disagree concerning the issue of eternal security, but that is not my primary point here. I am trying to make a distinction between two different issues. What determines whether I am related to another person is different from what determines whether I live in harmony with that person.

There is, however, a lot of scriptural support for the assurance of salvation. Paul asks in Romans 8:35: "Who shall separate us from the love of Christ?" He then answers that no created thing "shall be able to separate us from the love of God, which is in Christ Jesus our Lord" (Rom. 8:39). Jesus declared, "My sheep hear My voice . . . and I give eternal life to them, and they shall never perish; and no one shall snatch them out of My hand" (John 10:27-28). I am a born-again child of God, in spiritual union with Him by His grace, which I received through faith, not works. My relationship with God was settled when I was born into His family.

> ## WHEN I TRUST AND OBEY GOD, I LIVE IN HARMONY WITH HIM.

Is there anything I can do or not do that will interfere with the *harmony* of my relationship with God? Absolutely! Harmony with God is based on the same issues as harmony with my earthly father, which is trust and obedience. When I trust and obey God, I live in harmony with Him. When I do not respond properly to God, the harmony of our relationship is disturbed, and my life will reflect it; but I am still His child. I love my heavenly Father and want to live in harmony with Him, so I strive to live by faith according to what He says is true. Even when we fail to take Him at His Word or choose to walk by the flesh, our relationship with Him is not at stake, because we are related through the blood of Jesus Christ. The fact that we are not living a perfect life does not mean that we are no longer His children. This is more about God never leaving us or forsaking us than it is about our ability to hang on to God by our own effort.

THE TRUTH ABOUT OTHERS

Knowing who we are in Christ greatly impacts our lives and how we live. With the same reasoning, what we believe about others affects how we relate to them. In writing to the church in Corinth, Paul declared, "Great is my confidence in you; great is my boasting on your behalf" (2 Cor. 7:4). Paul said this to the church at Corinth with all its troubles! Is this just psychological hype? No, it is the truth. Paul knew that the work God had begun in the believers at Corinth would be completed. We are the recipients of God's positive regard, and we have the privilege to extend that to others. "Wherefore, accept one another, just as Christ also accepted us to the glory of God" (Rom. 15:7).

Tony Campolo tells a story about Teddy Stallard. Teddy was an unattractive, unmotivated child whose mother had died when he was in the third grade. Nobody liked Teddy, including his fifth grade teacher, Miss Thompson.

It was Christmastime of Teddy's fifth-grade year and the children in Miss Thompson's class brought her Christmas presents. They piled their gifts on her desk and crowded around to watch her open them. Among the presents was one from Teddy. She was surprised that he had brought her a gift. Teddy's gift was wrapped in brown paper and was held together with scotch tape. On the paper were written the simple words, "For Miss Thompson, from Teddy." When she opened Teddy's present, out fell a gaudy rhinestone bracelet, with half the stones missing, and a bottle of cheap perfume.

The other boys and girls began to giggle and smirk over Teddy's gifts, but Miss Thompson at least had enough grace to silence them by immediately putting on the bracelet and putting some of the perfume on her wrist. Holding her wrist up for the other children to smell, she said, "Doesn't that smell lovely?" And the children, taking their cue from the teacher, readily agreed with oohs and aahs.

At the end of the day when school was over and the other children had left, Teddy lingered behind. Slowly he came over to her desk and said softly, "Miss Thompson, you smell like my mother, and her bracelet looks real pretty on you, too. I'm glad you like my presents." When Teddy left, Miss Thompson got down on her knees and asked God to forgive her.

The next day, when the children came to school, a new teacher welcomed them. Miss Thompson had become a different person. She was no longer just a teacher, she had become an agent of God. She helped all the children, especially the slow ones, particularly Teddy Stallard. Teddy showed a dramatic improvement. He caught up with most of the students and even moved ahead of some.

The years passed. Miss Thompson did not hear from Teddy for a long time. Then one day, she received a note that read:

Dear Miss Thompson,
I want you to be the first to know. I will be graduating second in my class.
Love, Teddy Stallard

Four years later another note came:

Dear Miss Thompson,
They just told me I will be graduating first in my class. I wanted you to be the first to know. The university has not been easy, but I like it.
Love, Teddy Stallard

And four years later:

Dear Miss Thompson,
As of today, I am Theodore Stallard, M.D. How about that? I wanted you to be the first to know. I am getting married next month, the 27th to be exact. I want you to come sit where my mother would sit if she were alive.

You are the only family I have now: Dad died last year.

Love, Teddy Stallard

Miss Thompson went to that wedding and sat where Teddy's mother would have sat. She deserved to sit there; she had done something for Teddy that he could never forget.[2]

A pastor once asked me how people get to candidate at larger churches when a senior pastor leaves. He told me that he sends his resume to all these churches, but he never gets any response. I asked why he wanted out of his present church. He said, "The denominational leader talked me into being a candidate at this church several years ago, thinking it would be a great fit, but it isn't. This church is full of losers."

The church was full of God's children, not losers. It makes me wonder what the church members thought of him. The beloved Ethel Waters used to say, "God doesn't make any junk." As important as it is for us to believe who we are in Christ, it is equally important that we perceive other Christians in the same way and treat them accordingly. If we see people as losers, we will probably treat them that way. If we believe our brothers and sisters in Christ are redeemed saints, we will treat them as saints, and they will be greatly helped in behaving as saints.

As a ninth grader, Rick was the smallest guy in his high school. At five-feet tall and 90 pounds, he was the perfect candidate for the lightest weight class on the school's wrestling team. Rick started out as the junior varsity lightweight but moved to the varsity position when the boy at that spot moved away.

Rick's first year was not one for the record books. Of the six varsity matches he wrestled, he was pinned six times.

Rick had a dream of someday being a good enough wrestler to receive his varsity letter. He also wanted the school letterman's jacket to go with it. An athlete's letter and jacket seemed impossible though, because the jacket cost 100 dollars, which he could not afford, and his shot at earning the letter seemed slim.

Whenever Rick would share his dream of lettering in wrestling, most of his friends and teammates just laughed.

Every day after school, Rick was in the weight room, trying to build up his strength, or running the stadium bleachers, trying to increase his endurance, or in the wrestling room, trying to improve his technique.

The one person who continually believed in Rick was his grandmother. Every time she saw him, she told him to keep focused on his goal. Over and over again, she quoted Scripture verses to him, such as "I can do all things through Him [Christ] who gives me strength" (Phil. 4:13).

The day before the next season began, Rick's grandmother passed away. He was heartbroken. If he ever did reach his goal of someday getting a high school letter, his grandmother would never know.

That season Rick's opponents faced a new person. They expected easy victories. Instead, they got a battle. Rick won nine of his first ten matches.

Midway through the season, Rick's coach called him into his office to inform him that he would receive his high school letter. Rick was ecstatic. The only thing that could have made him feel better would have been the possibility of sharing it with his grandmother. If only she knew!

The coach smiled and presented Rick with an envelope. The letter had Rick's name on it, written in his grandmother's handwriting. He opened it and read:

Dear Rick,

    I knew you could do it! I set aside $100 to buy you a school jacket to put your letter on. I hope you wear it proudly, and remember, "You can do all things through Christ who gives you strength!"

Congratulations, Grandma

After reading the letter, the coach reached behind him and pulled out a brand new jacket with the school letter attached and Rick's name embroidered on the front. Rick realized that his grandmother did know after all.[3]

If we could memorize one verse in the Bible and never violate it, most of our problems would disappear in our homes and

> WE CAN BE PART OF GOD'S CONSTRUCTION CREW OR A MEMBER OF SATAN'S WRECKING CREW SIMPLY BY THE USE OF OUR WORDS.

churches. The verse is Ephesians 4:29: "Let no unwholesome word proceed from your mouth, but only such a word as is good for edification according to the need of the moment, that it may give grace to those who hear." We have the capacity to give grace to others by what we say to them. We can be part of God's construction crew or a member of Satan's wrecking crew simply by the use of our words. We can bless or curse others.

SINNERS IN THE HANDS OF AN ANGRY GOD

When I was in the eighth grade, we had a program called Religious Day Instruction. Every Tuesday afternoon the afternoon classes were shortened so that we could go to the church of our choice for the last hour of the day. It was not forced religion; students could choose to go to study hall. I went to the church of my mother's choice! One nice fall day, I decided to skip Religious Day Instruction. I played in the park and came back in time to catch the bus for my ride home to the farm. I thought I had gotten away with it.

I did not! The next day the principal called me in and chewed me out. Then he said, "I have arranged for you to be home Thursday and Friday." I was shocked. Expelled from school for two days for skipping Religious Day Instruction! I was not looking forward to seeing my parents, and the ride home was miserable. I thought about playing sick for two days or hiding in the woods when I should be in school. I could not act on those thoughts; rather, I knew I had to face my authority figures, but I was not looking forward to it. I went to my mother, because I knew there would be some mercy there. "Mom," I said, "I got expelled from school for two days for skipping Religious Day Instruction." At first she seemed surprised, and then she smiled and said, "Oh, Neil, I forgot to tell you. We called the school to see if you could stay home Thursday and Friday to help us pick corn."

If I had known that, would I have dreaded seeing my parents? Would the bus ride home have been miserable? Of course not, but I did not know that staying home Thursday and Friday was already justified. That is how many Christians live their lives. They live as though they are walking on glass. They cannot make any mistakes, because if they do, the hammer of God will fall on them.

Dear Christian reader, the hammer fell. It fell on Christ. He died once for all our sins (see Rom. 6:10). We are not sinners in the hands of an angry God. We are saints in the hands of a loving God who has called us to "draw near with a sincere heart in full assurance of faith, having our hearts sprinkled clean from an evil conscience and our bodies washed with pure water" (Heb. 10:22).

> For through Him [Christ] we both have our access in one Spirit to the Father. In whom we have boldness and confident access through faith in Him (Eph. 2:18; 3:12).

If you knew the truth, you would go running to your heavenly Father.

There are some Christian leaders who believe we should emphasize the sinful side of our human nature as a motivation to live righteously. I respectfully disagree. How can we motivate by guilt when "there is therefore now no condemnation for those who are in Christ Jesus" (Rom. 8:1). How can we motivate by fear when God has not given us a spirit of timidity but of power and love and discipline (see 2 Tim. 1:7). I believe we ought to tell everyone the truth about who they are in Christ and motivate them to live accordingly. To illustrate this truth, we close this little book with the following testimony from a missionary:

> Though I have been a Christian for many years, I never understood God's forgiveness and my spiritual inheritance. I have been struggling for years with a particular sin. I was in Bible college when I began this horrible practice. I never thought this living hell would ever end. I would have killed myself had I not thought that was a sin. I felt God had turned His back on me and I was doomed to hell because I couldn't overcome this sin. I hated myself. I felt like such a failure.
>
> The Lord led me to purchase your book *Victory over the Darkness*. I feel like a new Christian, like I've just been born again. My eyes are now open to God's love, and

I realize that I am a saint who has chosen to sin. I can finally say I am free, free of Satan's bondage and aware of the lies he has been feeding me.

I would confess to God and beg His forgiveness when I sinned, but the next time I fell deeper into Satan's grasp because I couldn't accept God's forgiveness and I couldn't forgive myself. I always thought the answer lied in drawing closer to God, but I went to Him in confusion, believing I was a sinner who couldn't be loved. *No more!* Through the Scriptures and the way you presented them to me, I am no longer a defeated Christian. I now know I am alive in Christ and dead to sin and a slave of righteousness. I now live by faith, according to what God said is true. Sin has no power over me. Satan has lost his grip on me.[4]

GOING DEEPER

1. What is grace?
2. What happened the day you were born again?
3. Why is the way we perceive one another so important?
4. What is the difference between seeing ourselves as sinners in the hands of an angry God and seeing ourselves as saints in the hands of a loving God? How does this affect your relationship with God?

AFTERWORD

For years, Freedom in Christ Ministries has been helping people all over the world discover who they are in Christ. It has been our prayer that the message in this book will do more than help you overcome a negative self-image. The truth should set you on the path of becoming all that God has created you to be. As we all learn to abide in Christ, we will bear good fruit.

However, many people hear the message of their identity and position in Christ but do not get it. For some reason, they just do not seem to connect with God. There is a good reason for this. In writing to the church at Corinth, Paul noted, "I gave you milk to drink, not solid food; for you were not yet able to receive it. Indeed, even now you are not yet able, for you are still fleshly. For since there is jealousy and strife among you, are you not fleshly, and are you not walking like mere men?" (1 Cor. 3:2-3). It would appear that jealousy and strife have to be resolved before Christians can even be able to receive the good news of their identity and position in Christ. In our experience, this has proven itself to be true.

Therefore, Freedom in Christ Ministries has been helping people all over the world resolve their personal and spiritual conflicts through genuine repentance and faith in God. The discipleship tool we use is titled *The Steps to Freedom in Christ*. The Steps can be purchased from many Christian bookstores or from our office. Many Christians can work through the process on their own. However, some cannot and need the help of a godly pastor or counselor. To know how to minister these Steps, read Neil's book *Discipleship Counseling* (Regal Books, 2003).

Helping Christians find their freedom in Christ requires a wholistic answer, which means we have to submit to God and resist the devil (see Jas. 4:7). It also requires an understanding and intentional inclusion of Christ and the Holy Spirit in the process. God is the wonderful counselor and the great physician. Only He can bind up the brokenhearted and set the captives free. He is the one who grants "repentance leading to the knowledge of the truth" (2 Tim. 2:25). Discipleship counseling has proven to be highly effective. Research has been conducted on this discipleship counseling process in several churches in conjunction with our Living Free in Christ conferences. The participants have been those who have requested further assistance after hearing the message, which is partially included in this book. They were given one extended counseling session with a trained encourager. A pretest was given, and then a posttest administered three months later indicated the following results:

57 percent improvement in depression
54 percent improvement in anxiety
49 percent improvement in fear
55 percent improvement in anger

50 percent improvement in tormenting thoughts
53 percent improvement in negative habits
56 percent improvement in their self-image

Christians connect with their loving heavenly Father after they have resolved their personal and spiritual conflicts. Every testimony you read in this book was a product of this repentance process. You too can find your freedom in Christ through genuine repentance and faith. When you do, your Bible will come alive, and you will grow in the grace of God. May the good Lord grant you that repentance.

Neil and Dave

For information on material and conferences contact
Freedom in Christ Ministries
9051 Executive Park Drive, Suite 503
Knoxville, TN 37923
Phone: (865) 342-4000
Fax: (865) 342-4001
E-mail: info@ficm.org
Website: www.ficm.org

NOTES

Chapter 1

1. Stephen Knight, "Steroid free-for-all? Maybe," *sportsnet.ca*, (November 18, 2002). www.sportsnet.ca/nfl/story/10376258592676.shtml (accessed March 7, 2003).
2. William Ernest Henley, "In Memorium R. T. Hamilton Bruce (Invictus)," st. 4.
3. Dave Dravecky, *When You Can't Come Back* (Grand Rapids, MI: Zondervan Publishing House, 1992), p. 125.
4. Ibid., p. 126.
5. David Meyers, quoted in Eric L. Johnson and Stanton Jones, eds., *Psychology and Christianity* (Downers Grove, IL: InterVarsity Press, 2000), p. 63.

Chapter 2

1. Source unknown.
2. Source unknown.
3. John Eldredge, *The Journey of Desire* (Nashville, TN: Thomas Nelson Publishing, 2000), p. 9.
4. Josh McDowell, *His Image, My Image* (San Bernardino, CA: Here's Life Publishing, 1984), p. 33.
5. Paul Tillich, *Shaking the Foundations* (New York: Peter Smith Publishing, 1990), n.p.

Chapter 3

1. Robert Jay Morgan, *More Real Stories for the Soul* (Nashville, TN: Thomas Nelson, 2000), p. 134.
2. Jim Burns, *No Compromise* (Ventura, CA: Regal Books, 2001), p. 28.
3. Neil Anderson and Rich Miller, *Freedom from Fear* (Eugene, OR.: Harvest House Publishers, 1999).
4. Ibid., p. 259.
5. Neil Anderson and Hal Baumchen, *Finding Hope Again* (Ventura, CA: Regal Books, 1999), n.p.
6. Neil Anderson, *Who I Am in Christ* (Ventura, CA: Regal Books, 2001), p. 278.

Chapter 4

1. Robert Jay Morgan, *More Real Stories for the Soul* (Nashville, TN: Thomas Nelson, 2000), p. 147.
2. Ibid., pp. 147-149.
3. Ibid., p. 149.

Chapter 5

1. Neil Anderson and Robert Saucy, *God's Power at Work in You* (Eugene, OR: Harvest House Publishers, 2001), pp. 25-27.
2. Confrontation with the righteousness and holiness of God frequently brought deep acknowledgment of one's own sinful condition. Peter's recognition of himself before the Lord as a "sinful man" is not uncommon among the saints (Luke 5:8; see also Gen. 18:27; Job 42:6; Isa. 6:5; Dan. 9:4-5). The believer is sinful, but Scripture does not seem to define his identity as a sinner.
3. John Stott, *God's Good News for the World* (Downers Grove, IL: InterVarsity Press, 1994), p. 187.
4. Ibid.

Chapter 7

1. For a greater understanding of these terms and the doctrine of sanctification see Neil Anderson and Robert Saucy, *God's Power at Work in You* (Eugene, OR: Harvest House, 2001).
2. E. K. Simpson and F. F. Bruce, *Commentary on the Epistles to the Ephesians and the Colossians* (Grand Rapids, MI: Eerdmans, 1957), p. 273.
3. Anthony A. Hoekema, *Created in God's Image* (Grand Rapids, MI: Eerdmans/Paternoster, 1986), p. 110.

Chapter 8

1. Wayne Rice, *More Hot Illustrations for Youth* (Grand Rapids, MI: Zondervan Publishing House, 1995), pp. 142-143.
2. Anthony Campolo, *Who Switched the Price Tags?* (Dallas, TX: Word

Publishing, 1987), pp. 67-72.

3. Rice, *More Hot Illustrations for Youth*, pp. 75-77.

4. Personal correspondence with Neil Anderson, date unknown.

Books and Resources by
Dr. Neil T. Anderson

About Dr. Neil T. Anderson

Dr. Neil T. Anderson was formerly the chairman of the Practical Theology Department at Talbot School of Theology. In 1989, he founded Freedom in Christ Ministries, which now has staff and offices in various countries around the world. In 2001, Dr. Anderson stepped down as president of Freedom in Christ Ministries and officially retired in May 2005 in order to start Discipleship Counseling Ministries. The purpose of this new ministry is to give greater focus to his personal speaking and writing ministry and to allow him more flexibility to serve others without financial constraints. For more information about Dr. Anderson and his ministry, visit his website at www.disciple shipcounselingministries.org.

Core Message and Materials

Victory Over the Darkness with study guide, audiobook and DVD (Regal Books, 2000). With over 1,000,000 copies in print, this core book explains who you are in Christ, how to walk by faith in the power of the Holy Spirit, how to be transformed by the renewing of your mind, how to experience emotional freedom, and how to relate to one another in Christ.

The Bondage Breaker with study guide, audiobook (Harvest House Publishers, 2000) and DVD (Regal Books, 2006). With over 1,000,000 copies in print, this book explains spiritual warfare, what our protection is, ways that we are vulnerable, and how we can live a liberated life in Christ.

Discipleship Counseling with DVD (Regal Books, 2003). This book combines the concepts of discipleship and counseling and teaches the practical integration of theology and psychology for helping Christians resolve their personal and spiritual conflicts through repentance and faith in God.

Steps to Freedom in Christ and interactive videocassette (Regal Books, 2004). This discipleship counseling tool helps Christians resolve their personal and spiritual conflicts.

Helping Others Find Freedom in Christ DVD (Regal Books, 2007). In this DVD package, Neil explains the seven Steps to Freedom and how to apply them through discipleship counceling. It gives a thorough explanation of the biblical basis for the steps and helps viewers understand the root cause of personal and spiritual problems.

Beta: The Next Step in Your Journey with Christ (Regal Books, 2004) is a discipleship course for Sunday School classes and small groups. The kit includes a teacher's guide, a student guide and two DVDs covering 12 lessons and the Steps to Freedom in Christ. This course is designed to enable new and stagnant believers to resolve personal and spiritual conflicts and be established alive and free in Christ.

The Daily Discipler (Regal Books, 2005). This practical systematic theology is a culmination of all of Neil's books covering the major doctrines of the Christian faith and the problems they face. It is a five-day-per-week, one-year study that will thoroughly ground believers in their faith.

Victory Over the Darkness Series

Overcoming a Negative Self-Image, with Dave Park (Regal, 2003)
Overcoming Addictive Behavior, with Mike Quarles (Regal, 2003)
Overcoming Doubt (Regal, 2004)
Overcoming Depression, with Joanne Anderson (Regal, 2004) and DVD (2007)

Bondage Breaker Series

Praying by the Power of the Spirit (Harvest House Publishers, 2003)
Finding God's Will in Spiritually Deceptive Times (Harvest House Publishers, 2003)
Finding Freedom in a Sex-Obsessed World (Harvest House Publishers, 2004)

Specialized Books

God's Power at Work in You, with Dr. Robert Saucy (Harvest House Publishers, 2001). A thorough analysis of sanctification and practical instruction on how we grow in Christ.

Released from Bondage, with Judith King and Dr. Fernando Garzon (Thomas Nelson, 2002). This book has personal accounts of defeated Christians with explanatory notes of how they resolved their conflicts and found their freedom in Christ, and how the message of Discipleship Counseling can be applied to therapy with research results.

Daily in Christ, with Joanne Anderson (Harvest House Publishers, 2000). This popular daily devotional is also being used by thousands of Internet subscribers every day.

Who I Am in Christ (Regal Books, 2001). In 36 short chapters, this book describes who you are in Christ and how He meets your deepest needs.

Freedom from Addiction, with Mike and Julia Quarles (Regal Books, 1997). Using Mike's testimony, this book explains the nature of chemical addictions and how to overcome them in Christ.

One Day at a Time, with Mike and Julia Quarles (Regal Books, 2000). This devotional helps those who struggle with addictive behaviors and explains how to discover the grace of God on a daily basis.

Freedom from Fear, with Rich Miller (Harvest House Publishers, 1999). This book explains anxiety disorders and how to overcome them.

Extreme Church Makeover, with Charles Mylander (Regal Books, 2006). This book offers guidelines and encouragement for resolving seemingly impossible corporate conflicts in the church and also provides leaders with a primary means for church growth—releasing the power of God in the church.

Experiencing Christ Together, with Dr. Charles Mylander (Regal Books, 2006.) This book explains God's divine plan for marriage and the steps that couples can take to resolve their difficulties.

Christ Centered Therapy, with Dr. Terry and Julie Zuehlke (Zondervan Publishing House, 2000). A textbook explaining the practical integration of theology and psychology for professional counselors.

Getting Anger Under Control, with Rich Miller (Harvest House Publishers, 1999). This book explains the basis for anger and how to control it.

The Biblical Guide to Alternative Medicine, with Dr. Michael Jacobson (Regal Books, 2003). This book develops a grid by which you can evaluate medical practices, and then applies the grid to the world's most recognized philosophies of medicine and health.

Breaking the Strongholds of Legalism, with Rich Miller and Paul Travis (Harvest House Publishers, 2003). An explanation of legalism and how to overcome it.

Free, with Dave Park (Regal Books, 2005). A 40-day devotional on sanctification.

To purchase the above material, contact the following:

Freedom In Christ Ministries
9051 Executive Park Drive,
Suite 503
Knoxville, Tennessee 37923
(866) 462-4747
info@ficm.org

E-3 Resources
317 Main Street, Suite 207
Franklin, Tennessee 37064
(888) 354-9411
info@e3resources.org

For ministry information, visit
www.discipleshipcounselingministries.org

Contact Freedom in Christ Ministries at the following:
Freedom in Christ Ministries
9051 Executive Park Drive, Suite 503
Knoxville, TN 37923
Telephone: (866) 462-4747
E-mail: info@ficm.org
Website: www.ficm.org

For product, contact:
E-3 Resources
317 Main Street
Suite 207
Franklin, Tennessee 327064
(888) 354-9411
info@e3resources.org

Also visit
www.regalbooks.com